HOLY CRAP, WE'RE PREGNANT

Two Parents. Two Sides of the Story.

JAKE & PAGE FEHLING

Redwood Publishing, LLC

Printed in the United States of America

First Printing, 2020

ISBN 978-1-952106-50-7 (paperback)
ISBN 978-1-952106-51-4 (specialty print)
ISBN 978-1-952106-52-1 (ebook)

Library of Congress Cataloguing Number: 2020910791

Published by Redwood Publishing, LLC
Orange County, California
info@redwooddigitalpublishing.com
www.redwooddigitalpublishing.com

Book Design By:
- Cover: Michelle Manley, Graphique Designs, LLC
- Interior: Ghislain Viau

Artwork & Images:
- Front Cover Photo: Shutterstock ID: 1380692510
- Back Cover Photo: Weslie Woodley Photography
- Interior Images: Page 9, 28, 35, 51, 60, 76, 110, 127, 154, 167, 171, 174: Jake & Page personal collection / Page 71: ID 169322140 © Kukotaekaterina | Dreamstime.com

Disclaimer: This book is a collection of actual events as they happened in our lives (or as we remember them happening) and we've told it as truthfully as our memories permit. We lost a lot of sleep.

TABLE OF CONTENTS

Pre-Pregnancy — The Good Ole Days

First Trimester — Puke and Rally

Second Trimester — Wait, Is This Really Happening?

Third Trimester — Are We There Yet?

DEDICATION

This book is dedicated to Ford, Cal, and June. We couldn't have written it without you. Literally. We've gone from "holy crap, we're pregnant," to "holy crap, we're your parents!" We don't know how we got so lucky, but we're beyond grateful that we did. We love you guys the most.

We also want to acknowledge the overachievers of 2020. While the world locked down under the weight of a global pandemic, many of us picked up hobbies. Some of us learned how to bake banana bread. At least two of us finally finished writing a book. A whole bunch of you got pregnant.

Congratulations. You're really bad at social distancing. And thank you. You're our first customers.

PROLOGUE

FASTEN YOUR CAR SEAT(BELTS)

Holy crap, we're pregnant.

The end.

There is obviously more to it, but those few words perfectly sum up how we felt when we saw that first positive pregnancy test. The second time around, we knew for a fact we were still careening through an "is-this-really-happening-we-can't-believe-we're-responsible-for-tiny-human-beings" haze. After the third? Well, we blacked out upon delivery, so, yeah, "Holy crap, we're pregnant," is about right.

Now, we know what you're asking yourself: Are these the words of confident, successful, responsible parents? Adults whose recommendations on preparing for and dealing with pregnancies I should trust? Two tireless (LOL) forty-somethings who feel the need to regurgitate all of their, well, regurgitations along the way? People from whom I'd take pregnancy advice?

Youbetcha.

So with that, we introduce . . . wait for it . . .

Holy Crap, We're Pregnant

Two parents. Two sides of the story.

"HCWP," as we'll refer to it going forward, may sound like one of the 374 disease acronyms your doctor scares you with before and after your child is born, but it's actually a she said/he said, slightly exaggerated, definitely sarcastic, hopefully humorous take on bringing a baby into this world.

Pregnancy isn't network TV, people. It's HBO. Carrying and delivering a baby involves profanity. And nudity. Lots of nudity. And not good, 3:00 a.m., old-school Skinemax nudity. We're talking, "I didn't even know my wife had that body part" nudity. It's a test of wills for the parents. You're teammates, but you sometimes hate each other. You're like Tony and Carmela Soprano. Except no one gets whacked.

(That's what she said.) Sorry. We had to.

The idea for HCWP came early. As we began to navigate our first pregnancy, we, like most new soon-to-be-parents, dove headfirst into books that ultimately scared our pants off. And since our pants being off is what got us here in the first place, that was a particularly impressive feat.

Most of the books we read were relatively entertaining, helped answer our questions, tastefully made light of some touchy and personal issues, and generally helped us get a better grasp on what exactly was happening to Page's body and Jake's anxiety levels.

When we would compare notes, however, we often came to the same conclusion: the books were either too serious or too technical. We also noticed a huge discrepancy between what was available for men versus women. While there are more books for women than you can shake a pee stick at, there isn't a whole helluva lot of quality stuff out there for guys.

Jake will be the first to admit that the line we hear a lot from men, *"But there's nothing out there for us guys, honey!"* is a bit dramatic. What's not overblown is that there isn't a lot of *good* stuff out there for men. And we're trying to make both the ladies *AND* their baby daddies truly learn and laugh. And cry. But not laugh-crying. More like, "this is probably the last night for a while that you'll have time to watch TV" crying.

With that in mind, we kept HCWP simple. We break the three trimesters down into key benchmarks; then we each offer our take. Every chapter is written from both perspectives, and rarely do we remember things exactly the same way. Since Page is the only one who directly went through the pregnancies, hers are the most accurate memories. She has, however, graciously allowed Jake to weigh in from his perspective, too. As long as she has the chance to respond at the end of each chapter to correct him. Also, Page wrote most of this paragraph. And she is beautiful, and smart, and the far better dancer between her and Jake.

Where were we?

Ahhh, yes . . . so, as soon as we found out we were pregnant, Page started a blog through her job at WNCN, the (then) NBC affiliate in Raleigh, North Carolina. She called it *The Preggo Page.*

The response was instantly positive. She attracted followers very quickly and her blog was often one of the top-viewed pages on the station's website.

Then . . . she got laid off. During her maternity leave. *Ouch.* Leaving Page pissed, and, well, let's just say she wasn't exactly in a blogging mood. When the dust settled and we hit some semblance of a stride with our first son, we decided the blog needed to be resuscitated, and this time, dad got involved. Months later, when Page was re-hired by WNCN (*dusts shoulders off*), we launched @ThePreggoPage (later it became @FehlingParents—get it? We're *failing* at parenthood? No? K. We suck at puns, too.) and we began throwing around ideas for a book that both men *and* women would get a kick out of. Something that didn't sugarcoat topics like the removal of a mucus plug, but rather wrapped them all up in short, fun, digestible stories, and left you wanting more. Of the *stories*. Definitely not of the mucus plugs.

We should also warn you (much like we should have before the mucus plug reference) that this is not an in-depth, high-brow, other-fancy-hyphenated-words look into reproduction. If you want to know the Apgar score for your amniotic fluid and how it correlates to your pregnancy perineum (or what any of those words actually mean and why they do NOT belong in a sentence together), you've come to the wrong place. We don't even know what any of that stuff is. Clearly. If, however, you want to know if there are other couples out there who think it's funny to draw a face and mustache on a big preggo belly and go out as jumbo-headed Groucho Marx on Halloween, then you've come to the right place. We're your people.

At some point, we decided to quit ignoring the people who encouraged us to write a book, and to actually sit down and write one. And we listened so well, it took us almost a decade to do it. So . . . far too many years, and probably one too many pregnancies later (But she's *so* cute. And we really did want that girl!), here we are: a couple of first-time authors delivering our pregnancy book to the world.

We're keeping our fingers crossed that you'll like it. But not our legs. Because, clearly, that hasn't worked for us in the past.

PRE-PREGNANCY

The Good Ole Days

CHAPTER 1
The Way Things Were

SHE SAID

My old boss (a mother of three) used to always say, "I can't even remember what I used to do on the weekends before I had kids." How nice for her. Because I can . . . and they are fun memories. Really fun. Except, of course, for the ones I *can't* actually remember . . . which only means that those memories were the most fun of all.

Before Jake and I had kids, we lived a pretty spectacular life—even for your common everyday DINKs (dual income, no kids). When we first met in Manhattan, both of our jobs were entry level, but entry level in perk-laden fields. Our courtship was full of free tickets to shows and sporting events; hook-ups at restaurants; trips all over the world on the company's dime; and parties, after-parties, and after-after-parties that had us getting home at 5:00 a.m. on Saturday and Sunday mornings. I worked as an NBC page (yes, I was "Page-the-Page" . . . go ahead . . . I've heard it at least eight million times) on the *Weekend Today* show. Because my schedule was so weird, our first few dates were on Friday nights at 10:00 p.m. and would last clear through the night until I had to be at work the next morning at 4:00 a.m. We called them, "The 10 Spot." It was an old MTV term. Remember when you got to sit around and watch MTV? Yeah . . . neither do I.

We definitely lived it up while we were in New York. And after about a year of some of the most fun times of our lives, Jake proposed to me on the shore of the Hudson River, surprising me later that night with an engagement party at the place where we had our first "10 Spot." It had been about a year since we'd first met, and it's a good thing he didn't drag his feet anymore because I already had two dresses and a church booked by the time he popped the question. Hey, when you know, you know.

After about a year of squeezing both of our oversized selves and our morbidly obese cat into (what at least felt like) a 200-square-foot apartment, we decided we were sick of living like we were still in college. So, ironically enough, we moved back down to Raleigh, North Carolina, which was within tobacco spittin' distance from where we both went to college: UNC Chapel Hill. It was there in Raleigh that we started to get the itch.

If you've never been to North Carolina and you don't want kids (yet, or at all), don't go there. Because you'll drive into town in your sports car and designer clothes, and leave wearing . . . well, it doesn't even matter what you have on because it will be unrecognizable under all the baby spit up. And you'll be driving a minivan. This state—with its beach on one side and mountains on the other, affordable housing, good schools, college sports rivalries, mild weather—makes people want to reproduce so more people can enjoy the family-friendly lifestyle.

The fact that my brother and sister-in-law had a one-year-old, and my three best friends from high school were all either knocked up or weaning their first kid, didn't help either. My competitive side was kicking in. I couldn't let all these people beat us in the kid race! And then there was our first all-married adults Christmas at Jake's parents' house. Nothing is more vanilla than a holiday meal with no corn being thrown your way from the kids' table in the corner of the room. So, basically, I decided I was ready to have kids because I needed something to entertain us by next Christmas.

If only I had just asked for a portable DVD player instead . . .

HE SAID

"You've totally got to meet my roommate!"

I remember it like it was yesterday. I had moved to Hoboken, New Jersey, a few days prior and was sitting in front of the one person I knew in Manhattan. And by "knew," I mean we had one class together at UNC. I think she'd seen my thirty-eight desperate emails earlier that week about getting together for drinks and decided to adopt me for her community service hours for the week. And hours it was, as we sat there from about nine in the evening till midnight, throwing down drinks and apps to the tune of about $300. I quickly learned that my "$1 PBR Nights" from North Carolina not only didn't exist in New York, but also, that in NYC, one dollar doesn't even get you a coaster. Upon saying goodbye at the end of the night, and after seeing that I'd passed the only two prerequisites of standing taller than six feet (I'm six-foot-five) and professing love for salsa dancing (that might have been a lie), she decided that I was a fit for her roommate.

Now, you should know that I had spent the previous few years since college bouncing from one setup, blind date, train wreck of a story to another, so the idea of meeting yet another roommate had me even less excited than I was to see the bill that night. Come on, it's the Big Apple—where better else to be newly single?! Nevertheless, I acquiesced and agreed to meet this roommate at an alumni event two weeks later.

Maybe it was because I was near-blackout by the end of that first night, but I must have missed the details that the roommate was six feet tall and blonde, and celebrates Jim Carrey's entire body of work, because that's exactly who I met at this event. Good Lord. I'd never really bought into love at first sight prior to that, but, "You're telling me there's a chance!" Yes. Yes, there was, Jim.

At the beginning of the night, we were surrounded by friends who were there only to help bridge any awkward gaps in conversation. By the end of it, we were obnoxiously giggling like schoolgirls, in a back booth of a nearby bar . . . until I eventually pushed my finger against her lips and whispered, "Just go. . ."

Within a week, I was making mix CDs for her. I know. We were hanging out incessantly—to the sheer joy of her two roommates in their postage stamp–sized Upper East Side apartment—and I was blind to the fact that traveling from my place to her apartment each night after work *AND THEN BACK TO MY PLACE AT LIKE 3:00 A.M.* was, well, insane. Not to mention the fact that it made my already three-hour-round-trip work commute more like five. I was, to put it mildly, in love.

A little less than a year later, it was time to *really* DTR.

"So . . . like . . . um, what are we doing?" she asked.

The first road bump/potential drama/hiccup/whatever you want to call it in the most blissful nine months of my life.

"What do you mean?" I replied, anxiety-ridden.

"I mean . . . with us. Where do you see this going?"

"Well, we could go grab a bagel down the street or—"

"No, you idiot . . . like, marriage."

I, of course, knew where she was going, and to be honest, despite my weak attempt to play dumb, I was ready, too.

"Oh, yeah . . . well, I mean . . . like, I'm ready . . . or I think I'm ready, you know? I mean, like, what do you think? You want to do this?"

We were registering at Target by noon. She was adding sheets to the list. I was debating how many Nintendo Wiis we should ask for. We were off to an amazing start.

By the grace of God, and in a move that surely added years to my Lincoln Tunnel–fearing life, she decided to move out to Hoboken with me after we got married. We lived in a small apartment with a view of Manhattan. We adopted a cat. We went to the gym. We hung out with friends. We brought wine to BYOB restaurants with sidewalk seating. We ate burritos. A lot of burritos. It was heaven.

After about a year, though, we got the itch. You see, New York was my fifth stop on a madly-trying-to-climb-the-ladder job tour since college, and Page was coming off two years in the Peace Corps and one more in DC. We fancied ourselves movers and shakers, and after twelve months, it was time to roll. Page made the call—"I want to try the TV thing"—and with that, we were off. Back to North Carolina . . .

. . . And into the WHAT ARE YOU WAITING FOR, HAVE BABIES ALREADY vortex of the South. Maybe it's tradition, parental pressure, or the water, but it's what people do down there.

Needless to say, it wasn't long before we started talking about starting to try for some kiddos of our own.

"How many?" Page would ask.

"No more than two," I would mutter with no clue or feeling one way or another. A couple kids seemed about right (I have one brother and two half-brothers I'm close to, and Page has one brother), but I could definitely envision three. Page? Give her all da babies. She wanted a TLC show's worth of children.

So there we were, sitting in bed, asking ourselves the same vague questions we were asking each other two years earlier:

"So . . . like . . . um, what are we doing?"

"What do you mean?" I replied, anxiety-ridden.

"I mean . . . with kids. Where do you see this going?"

"Oh, yeah, well, I mean . . . like, I'm ready . . . or I think I'm ready, you know? I mean, like, what do you think?

"You want to do this?"

THE WAY THINGS WERE — SHE REACTS

This is probably the one chapter where Jake will actually have more to say than I do. And I'm not even remotely complaining, because most of it was about how we met and fell in love . . . over Dumb and Dumber. *And then we had three kids in four years.*

Who knew Jim Carrey was so prophetic?

THE WAY THINGS WERE — HE REACTS

Wow, so, OK, that made me cry. Not in the sense of, "Awww, that's so sweet, Page," but rather, "Jesus H., we had a good thing going. Remind me: Why did we have kids again?!" And seriously, let's pour one out for Farley (our cat). Man, I loved Farls. Until we got pregnant and everyone scared the shit out of us: "You have a litter box in the house with your pregnant wife? Why don't you start a gas leak while you're at it." Farley was gone that afternoon—off to "summer camp" at Page's parents' house. Sad day? Tough decision? Yes and yes. But c'mon, tiny humans > fat cats.

Our first baby, Farley. We should have quit while we were ahead.

CHAPTER 2
Trying

SHE SAID

So it's officially unofficial. You are not trying not to get pregnant. I mean . . . you are *not* not trying to not get pregnant. What I mean is, you are not trying to not get pregnant. So you are trying to get pregnant.

Sort of.

WHAT in the world does "trying" to get pregnant mean anyway, though? Well, apparently, it depends on who you ask. To me, "trying" implied we were actively pedal-to-the-metal, balls-to-the-wall (figuratively speaking) "trying" to make a baby—like, now. Today. And every day until it actually happened. I didn't like to think of us as "trying," because if you are "trying" to do something and you don't do it, then you have failed. If you're not "trying" and you happen to get pregnant, then oops . . . you're just lucky. Again, depending on who you ask. But if you're not there yet, don't worry. Hopefully, you will be. And if you're reading this book, then maybe you are already. Thinking of yourself as lucky, that is. And thinking of yourself as having "tried." Is anyone else confused right now?

When Jake and I decided a baby might be somewhere in our near future, my doctor recommended I go ahead and stop taking my birth control pills a few months before we started "trying." I guess to let things just get back to normal and get all those birth control hormones and drug effects oonched out of there before a kiddo would take over my womb area. There are surely scientific reasons for this, but as you will quickly learn in this book, we are not scientific people, and oonching un-baby-friendly stuff out of my body was reason enough for me.

I should tell you that at this point, I was ready and willing to full-on go for it. Jake, not so much. I think he was still trying to wrap his brain around the amount of fantasy football leagues he would have to win to pay for just one semester's worth of books when this future kid went to future college. So, one day, I told him straight up that I was good to go whenever he was, and the ball was in his court. AND (listen up here, ladies) that I would really let it be in his court until he was ready, and to just let me know when that was. Yep, I was just patiently waiting away for *annnnnny* day now when he wanted to start "trying."

I started having visions of an evening when he would surprise me with flowers, take me to a spectacularly romantic dinner with amazing views of the city, get down on one knee, and tell me he was ready to create another human being with me that he hoped had my eyes and his back hair. Or something like that.

Fast-forward a few months to one night when Jake and I decide it's time to try out a Greek restaurant close to our house. We sit outside on their patio and gorge ourselves on two bottles of chardonnay (don't judge), falafel platters, gyros (which Jake insists on pronouncing the "correct" way—"YEE-doh"—all night (please judge), and enough hummus to coat the Parthenon.

Not one to be dissuaded from a date-night booty call, Jake makes it clear when we get home that, even though I feel like the poster child for *My Big Fat Greek Wife,* he'd still like to end date night with a little make-out session. And it is in the middle of this fat-ass Greek sexual slopfest that he decides to tell me he's ready to "try." And what the hell do you know . . .

It actually worked.

HE SAID

OK, enough of the sappy crap. Let's move on to some hardcore dude stuff, like . . .

. . . trying to get pregnant.

Right.

C'mon, you bought this book, so you know what you're getting into. Or, hell, maybe you don't. You could still be in the first trimester when your wife isn't showing yet, isn't really experiencing the whole morning- sickness thing, and is still interested in a post–8:30 p.m. bedtime. LOLOLOLOLOLOL! Ahem . . . sorry.

Not to worry, though, I'm here to help walk you through all the chocolate-covered-salmon grocery store runs and every one of those 8,125 foot rubs.

Let's start with how we got into this whole mess to begin with.

I'll be the first to say, I still have no clue what the difference is between "trying" and "just seeing what happens." Doesn't seem like there is a difference, but apparently there is. A YUGE one.

Let's play a little game. I'll give you a phrase or situation, and you guess whether it's called "trying" or "just seeing what happens." Here goes:

"We pulled the goalie last night."

"I'm off the pill."

"We just had irresponsible sex with zero protection."

Trying, right? Wrong. God, you're such an idiot.

Welcome to my world. Page was convinced that it was going to take us eleven years to conceive, so she was über-conservative when it came to defining the whole thing. I once made the mistake of mentioning to some close friends over dinner one night that we were trying. Page retaliated with a swift spork to my thigh and a little Destiny's Child karaoke: "*No, no, no, no, no*—hahaha!—he's kidding. What he meant to say was that we're just seeing what happens."

Huh?

Turns out, you're only trying if—and *only* if—you define it to your friend as something along these lines: "Funny you should ask, Janice. I've been checking my vagina hourly, examining the adhesiveness of the secretions, and if the coefficient of the compound offers an acutely strong resistance, and the moon is showing as four-sevenths full, then there is an 84 percent chance I'm ovulating, and as such, I will be ordering my husband to have missionary-style intercourse in an attempt to impregnate me. I am excited to now officially be trying."

Seriously. One of her Catholic friends did that. Are you freaking kidding me?

Forgive me for being a dumb man, but come on; when you pull Ole' Marty Brodeur, jump off the BCPs, and return to the rare-air frequency of honeymoon sex, then guess what? YOU'RE TRYING.

Finally, one morning (or was it an evening . . . shit, do I have to remember the date?), as I gracefully prepared to deliver some really jaw-dropping, awe-inspiring, let's be honest below-average sex, I nervously asked Page if she wanted to go for it.

Truly, I think I literally blurted out, "Hey, let's go for it."

She looked at me, confused. I was certain I had blown it. No kids for you, Fehling. Well done.

"Go for what," she asked. "Food? Wait . . . are you talking about sex?"

So you're sayin' there's a chance.

"Yes. Wait, no, not food, but yes, sex . . . but sure, I'd actually love some food too . . . but first, sex, like, um . . . with kids in mind. Wait, sorry, no, that came out wrong. Let's have some kids."

She looked at me in disbelief—one, because I was actually offering this idea myself, and two, because she couldn't believe I was dumb enough to think we could just flip a switch and have a kid. It took her about a tenth of a second to warm to the idea though, and with no perfect moon, no Jodeci, and only a little bit of adhesiveness, we threw all caution to the wind.

Seven seconds later, the boys were swimmin'.

TRYING — SHE REACTS

All I know is, we "tried," and it worked. Or did it? I guess that's the question to examine in the next book in the Holy Crap *series:* Holy Crap . . . What Do We Do with This Thing Now That It's Here?!"

And hey, you know something I didn't know about myself? Apparently, I got some foot rubs—8,125 of them, I hear—from Jake while I was pregnant! They must have been post-8:30 p.m. while I was asleep in a pool of chocolaty salmon, because I don't remember a single one.

OPA!

TRYING — HE REACTS

OMG, the Greek restaurant.

I will say, going down this road again, even all these years and pregnancies later, made my brain hurt. You're either trying or you're not. And let me tell you, we were definitely trying on that beautiful night in "Athens." It was perfect. Your breath was laced with tzatziki. My burps reeked of hummus. "Me. You. Baby." I definitely **don't** *remember you saying.*

I mean—be honest—could Page and I sound any hotter right now? You couldn't find a more disgusting couple at this point if you . . . wait for it . . . TRIED.

Sees self out.

CHAPTER 3
Seeing Signs

SHE SAID

First of all, let me just say, we have already screwed you over with the title of this chapter. Why?

Because you should never be looking for a plus sign.

You should instead be looking for something much clearer. You should be looking for something that blatantly and very clearly tells you you're pregnant. You should be looking for something that reads . . . oh, I don't know . . . "PREGNANT?!." If someone had tipped Jake and me off on this, we would have saved at least $1,048 on at-home pregnancy tests.

The thing is (as the boxes say), a pregnancy test will tell you you're pregnant as early as five days before your missed period. But as it turns out, there *is* such a thing as being only a little bit pregnant . . . or, at least, having just a little bit of the pregnancy hormone. And if you, like me, want to know you're pregnant the minute the tadpole makes it inside the jellyfish, you will pee on a stick just early enough to thoroughly confuse the both of you.

I think the first time I peed on a stick our first go-round, I was due for my period within the week. I had bought a three-pack pregnancy test at CVS the night before and downed seventeen glasses of water on my way to bed so that I would be sure to be able to pee in the morning, which is when "they" say that the pregnancy hormone is the strongest. After five nighttime pee sessions, I officially woke up at 6:00 a.m. with a(nother) full bladder and practically knocked the poor little stick out of my hand with my Niagara Falls pee stream. The one we bought had a "test" line that shows you the test is working.

Two blue lines: pregnant.

One blue line: not pregnant.

No blue lines: faulty test. Or you did it wrong. And are officially too stupid to reproduce.

The test says you have to wait three minutes for the results to be official. So I spend all 180 seconds repeating the rules to Jake, who is trying to, A. fall back asleep and B. not wet the bed because I won't let him into the bathroom where the stick is, lest he cheat and look early, thereby ruining our chances at offspring. So there I am blabbering "two lines pregnant, one line not pregnant . . . two lines pregnant, one line not pregnant" on repeat until the God-blessed three minutes are mercifully up.

I, of course, can't handle the idea of seeing whatever it is on there, so I tell Jake to go in and pick up the stick and make him promise on our (soon to be?!) firstborn that he won't look until he's back out in the bedroom with me. When he comes out I perch on the edge of the tub, give him the go-ahead to sneak a peak . . .

then proceed to stare holes into the top of his skull as he studies the stick for at least seventeen hours before looking up at me and saying, "two lines pregnant, one line not pregnant, right?"

"Yes," I manage to choke out through gritted teeth and my best HAVEYOUNOTLISTENEDTOANEFFINGWORDIVE-BEENSAYINGSINCEIEMPTIEDMYBLADDERALLOVER-THATLITTLEPIECEOFSHITPLASTIC?!?!?! expression.

"Well, then, what the hell does one and a half mean?!" he responds.

And it actually was a damn good question.

I looked and had to agree: there was one clear-as-day blue line, and in the other circle, definitely a little something. It could just as easily have been a shadow from the light hitting it oddly as an indication that nine months from now, I'd be folded in half in a hospital gown, trying to see over my watermelon-sized boobs and trying my best not to poop on a table. But more on that later. Aren't you looking forward to the childbirth chapter now?

Three tests later, we were more confused than ever. For those of you keeping score at home, we were now looking at:

One-line pregnancy tests: zero

Two-line pregnancy tests: zero

One-and-a-half-line pregnancy tests: three

And in all eighteen pages and seven languages of pregnancy test directions, there is not a single word in there about one and a half lines.

Well, what I now know is that even a small shadow—even a faint greenish-bluish-grayish squiggly something-or-other—means there is some pregnancy hormone being detected, and it counts as a line in that second circle. You are pregnant and probably also now partially blind from eyestrain. But that better be enough for you to believe it, because good luck getting your OB-GYN to see you before you are at least eight weeks, even though "this is your first baby and you reeeeeeeally want to be absolutely sure, and you're soooooooo excited that you can't possibly wait that long." Save it, sister. They've heard it all before. Now, I do have one good girlfriend who has lied and said she had some spotting and wanted to come in to make sure everything was all right. And that did get her in early for a confirmation. Although she's never been punished by way of miscarriages or any obvious birth defects, her three-year-old did just "redecorate" her entire living room with a set of Sharpie markers. If that's not karma coming back to bite her in the ass, then I don't know what is.

My advice is that if you, like me, will feel better with several confirmed sources even before your doc will see you, then go ahead and go to an urgent care center for a blood test or just splurge on the digital pee-stick version. Nothing quite makes it hit home like seeing the actual word *PREGNANT* pop up on a semi-circle an inch away from where you just urinated.

Huge life changes that come to you in the form of graphic bodily functions: welcome to parenthood.

HE SAID

So you've decided to start trying. And I mean *trying*. Now what?

It's time for the stick, is now what.

Ah, the pregnancy test pee stick. About six inches long, this unassuming piece of plastic can literally rock your world, change your life, eat you for dinner, and spit you back out in about three minutes flat.

Three minutes flat, that is, assuming you have 20/20 vision.

Let me explain.

The stick comes in one million shapes, sizes, and price points. You can buy one that shows a plus sign or one that pops up a second, parallel line. You can buy digital versions that, when positive, flash "Oh, snap!," or you can get one that, when programmed, plays a frantic video message from your overexcited in-laws. What did we go with? We pulled the trigger on a generic model from CVS that looked like it was whittled by a four-year-old. Because of course we did.

One night, about a month after we first bought said stick, the time had come. We figured what the hell, let's get our pee on. We agreed to run the test the next morning and let the babies, er, cards fall where they may. The alarm was set for 7:00 a.m. (Jesus, did we really use to have to set an alarm to wake up BY 7:00 a.m.?), and we fell fast asleep with visions of triplets dancing in our heads.

Jarred awake by the random, crackly country music station that Page refused to move the alarm dial from, we hustled to the bathroom where she tore open the stick's wrapper like a frantic Charlie Bucket.

Deep. Breaths.

Who are we kidding? We were FREAKING out. I want to come up with ways to describe the feeling to you, but honestly, I can't come close. The thing comes back positive, and you're smacked in the jaw by equal doses of euphoria, fear, and reality. If it's negative, all you get is frustration with a small side of relief.

Page heads into the bathroom. A few minutes later, she emerges, dripping stick in hand. So hot.

Now we're supposed to wait three minutes. You hear the cliché all the time, but this was the longest three minutes of our lives. If only I could remember what we did to pass the time—oh yeah, that's right: we pissed our collective pants (Page mustered up a contribution). We could not have possibly talked about anything even remotely rational. I honestly think that, overcome with anxiety and anticipation, I blacked out.

Ding!

The three minutes were up. We looked deeply into each other's eyes. This was it. The moment we barely planned for at all, yet were convinced we were ready for. We slowly look down at the stick, and . . .

"Oh my God . . ."

"OH MY GOD!"

"Wait . . ."

"Is that a second line?"

"Hold on . . . wait, yes . . . wait . . . let me get my glasses."

"Should we just assume that we've got two lines?"

"Dude, that is *so* a second line."

"What the fuck."

Let's just say that last line wasn't from me.

Unbelievable. We look at the box: two lines means you're pregnant. We look back at the stick. I swear—there are one and a half lines. There is, without question, something there. It appears to be a line, but one that by the looks of it, the pregnancy Gods tried to erase while we weren't looking. It's there, but it's about as faint as my heartbeat was ten seconds ago.

"Now what?" Page says to me, incredulously.

"I think we're supposed to call our family," I reply, stupidly.

"No," she says. "We're getting another test."

And with that, she's off to Walmart. For what, who knows. I half expected her to come back with the pharmacist. About twenty minutes go by, and I hear the garage door open. She's back, she's got another stick . . . and I've got a second mortgage.

The new stick? Ha! This was no stick, my friend. This was, for all intents and purposes, a laptop sized for vaginal entry. No way in hell this was a Rollback item. Must have cost five grand, easy. There was an LCD digital face, a Gucci leather padded handle, and hell, there was even a swatch of ShamWow included to clean up any residual urine. This was the Cadillac of sticks.

Wasting no time, Page flees to the bathroom where she unleashes fury once again. (*What did you drink, woman?!*) Three minutes later, in addition to a full-color, twenty-eight page binder complete with bar graphs and pie charts, we have a clear-as-day report from the stick: "YES."

Yes.

YES?

YES!!!

YEEEEEEEEOOOOOOHHH MY GOD.

SEEING SIGNS — SHE REACTS

And by "we" were scared shitless, Jake does not mean both of us. He was apprehensive, with a side of cautiously pleased. Obviously excited, but also realistic and responsibly thinking of the life changes we'd need to make over the next nine months. I, on the other hand, was off-the-charts elated. And one of the stupider people around, thinking only of warm, cuddly babies—and nothing of sleepless nights, vaginas that tear in half, and bleeding nipples. Thank goodness children have two parents.

SEEING SIGNS — HE REACTS

What a cluster that morning was. And to think once we'd (finally) determined that we were pregnant, I bolted out the door for work. I can only imagine what everyone in the office thought. Deer. In. Headlights.

"Wow, Jake must have misspelled a word in that press release this morning; he looks like hell."

"Yeah, either that, or he and Page just blew through two boxes of pregnancy tests, riding a roller coaster of emotion so bizarre that Jake can't possibly see straight, let alone realize that he's wearing mismatched shoes."

"Yeah . . . I'm gonna go with the press release."

Positive pregnancy test #1 (of 17) for our first pregnancy!

Positive pregnancy test for our second pregnancy... like five minutes later.

Positive Pregnancy Test #3. Exhausted. Zero Fs given
about pictures. Just trust us, we were pregnant.

FIRST TRIMESTER

Puke and Rally

CHAPTER 4
Tattletale

SHE SAID

If this is your first pregnancy and you're early in the game, then you're in that gloriously secretive state where your body isn't giving you away yet. Friends might be starting to wonder why you've "been on antibiotics and can't drink" for the past two months straight.

"Nasty ear infection I just can't kick!"

Coworkers might question the upchuck sounds coming from the last bathroom stall every morning

"Bulimia from my college days rearing its ugly head once again!"

Strangers on the street might be stopping you in your tracks—bless your heart—to give you their dermatologist's card.

No excuse needed for adult acne. People feel sorry enough for you and won't ask; trust me.

But if you're able to fool everyone with excuses for the symptoms and signs, you're in the clear, because your bod won't really start to change much to the naked eye until right around the second trimester. And then your eye is gonna be about the only thing you'll want to see naked. But we'll get to all that later.

Right now, you've got a decision to make: Who are you going to tell that you're pregnant? And when? How?

As with anything related to pregnancy, parts of this are super fun (like telling soon-to-be-grandparents that they're about to have retaliation ammo the next time Doris from down the street makes them watch her little grandson Bobby's "first poopy in the potty" video . . . *again*), and parts kinda suck (like . . . telling your boss).

The first time I got pregnant, we did a combination of things to break the news, including vague trying-to-be-clever notes in Father's Day cards, having a best friend's four-year-old make the announcement for us, and hosting garbled Skype videos. All of which basically culminated in me getting emotional and teary and blubbering my way somehow into the announcement that "We're pregnant!" Praise be. Both that we're pregnant, and that everyone finally now knows what four-year-old Drew meant when he yelled out, "Tia's gonna have Uncle Jake and play with our baby!" Huh? Exactly.

The second time I got pregnant, we thought we were slick. I bought a "Big Brother" shirt for our oldest, Ford (who at the time was only five months old, so good luck finding a "Big Brother" shirt for a kid who is not supposed to play that role yet), and had him wear it in front of every person to whom we wanted to break the news. Average pick-up-on-it time? Ranged anywhere from thirty minutes to not at all, until I held him up in front of their face and yelled, "What does his shirt say?!" And even then, they would stupidly read it off to themselves at least fifteen times (with me in the background nodding and rubbing my belly and Jake behind me fake humping from behind—hey, some people will just never guess unless you truly spell it out for them) before finally picking up on the fact that the shirt was conveying an actual message and wasn't just a random shout-out to bad reality TV.

Of course, the other thing to consider here is timing. And I'm gonna get serious here for just a minute. But just for literally one minute, don't worry. The standard rule that most people are comfortable with is to wait to tell the masses until you hit twelve weeks, as the chances of miscarriage plummet at that point. Our theory on that was always that we told people early on who were people that we would want to know even if something did happen and the pregnancy didn't last. To me (us), that's not the kind of thing we would have wanted to go through alone and from talking with friends who have gone through miscarriages it seems like they were glad to have close friends and family be in the know so they had people to talk with, pray with, and just generally live through that hard time with.

Miscarriage is, of course, something I hope none of you reading this book has had, or will have to deal with. But statistically speaking, it probably is. You and your baby daddy will want to factor that sort of thing in when you're deciding who to tell and when. Unless, of course, you throw up on your coworker's shoe for the fourth day in a row (like a friend of mine did FOUR TIMES during commercial breaks when she was anchoring the morning news and couldn't leave the desk to run to the bathroom), in which case, you're better off fessing up that you're pregnant rather than trying to come up with another excuse.

*Perhaps we should have tattooed it on
his forehead instead?*

HE SAID

You're pregnant. Bravo! Your penis and vagina jive well together. Penis, meet vagina. Vagina, penis. Wait, what? You already know each other? You just conceived a baby? Well, damn. Congrats!

Now, remember when you were a kid and someone told you something really juicy, only they paired that glorious nugget of knowledge with the impossible task of keeping it to yourself? "Don't tell anyone," they said. "Keep it a *secret*." Well, that's what this is. Except you're not a kid. You're a grown-ass adult, and you're all like, "I'm a grown-ass adult. I can make my own decisions and keep or not keep my own secrets."

Exceeeeeeept . . .

There's a rule that you can't tell people you're pregnant. Seriously, look it up. Not until you're "out of the weeds." Or until you're "done with the first trimester." Or until "your wife has stopped puking in the morning."

OK, ladies, I know you're about to spike this book into the toilet (assuming you're even reading my chapters to begin with), saying things like, "Do you not know what can happen in those first three months?!?" or, "Do you not know the risks out there that can lead to a mother losing a baby?" I promise, I'm not completely heartless. Or a moron. I get it. There are risks. But still, come on. Can't we just tell our *parents?*

That's what I ran by Page. Flash back a couple chapters (or years, in real life), and you'll remember that my wife and I are gun-jumpers of sorts. We like to put the cart before the proverbial horse. I thought that telling people we were pregnant like fifteen seconds after seeing the really faint kinda-sorta second line would be totally cool. Apparently, it's not cool. Apparently, I'm an idiot.

To be fair, Page eventually acquiesced early. Albeit eight to nine weeks later. Which is early, I'm told. In that time I think I lost ten pounds and added about ten times that many gray hairs trying to keep this thing bottled up.

Rules are made for a reason though. We're fortunate to have never had an issue in those first couple of months for any of our pregnancies, while we have had friends miscarry during that time. More friends than we would have ever thought before we started talking to people about this sort of thing. That said, I'm sure any couple that has lost a baby at least at some point shared these feelings of, well, wanting to share the news. It's only natural. Or maybe I'm just hoping you understand, and in reality, I'm just digging a deeper grave.

Land your plane, Fehling . . .

OK, to bring it home, fellas: You can't. You just can't. Don't tell your coworkers. Don't tell your mailman. And for the love of everything true and holy, don't tell your parents. Oh Jesus God, don't tell your parents. Because then she has to tell her parents, and then the parents have to tell their friends. Or their cousin Pat because they are far tighter with their cousin Pat than anyone else on the planet and cousin Pat has only let four or five (thousand) secrets slip over her life, so I'm sure she'll lock this one down.

And if you do let it slip? Ha! Enjoy the ride, and please keep your arms, legs, and reproductive organs inside the vehicle at all times. Here's the rundown: eight minutes later, one entire side of the family knows. Then the other. Then, "Whoops, I thought you said it was cool to put it on Facebook." Then, *knock, knock,* it's your neighbor, who wants to borrow some sugar and slap you on the ass because "Jake, I just saw a retweet that you and Page are pregnant with triplets that are due any day now." Have you ever played a game of dominoes and incorporated LSD, complete strangers, and the game "telephone?" Welcome to telling people that you're pregnant.

TATTLETALE — SHE REACTS

Wow. This was a tricky one. Both of us clearly felt the need to address the seriousness of at least one aspect of the "to tell or not to tell" dilemma. Jake's entire chapter pretty much revolved around it, and yet he still managed to start things off with the simulated introduction of a vagina and a penis. And this, dear reader, is why we thought it was a good idea that we present both the male and the female perspective throughout this book.

TATTLETALE — HE REACTS

Alrighty then. I had thought when I was typing my version of this chapter that I might be coming across as sounding like a bumbling, derailed idiot, and now, after reading Page's entry, I know I did. Sorry. She's right; getting people's hopes up too early is a tough road to go down. Point is, don't say anything until (your baby mama tells you) like twelve weeks in. Yeah, that sounds about right.

taps foot

OK, can we please move on, Page? If people wanted to read a serious chapter about first trimester horror stories, they would have bought one of those other, thicker books with quotes from "experts" and "doctors."

CHAPTER 5
The Name Game

SHE SAID

What's in a name? Everything.

Don't even say it, because no, it's not too early to start thinking about names.

"But we're only in Chapter 5," you say. "Shouldn't we first talk about morning sickness and cravings and how to tie your shoes when you can't reach your feet?"

No.

Why? Because all of those things pass. You will eventually be able to get out of bed without first downing an entire sleeve of Saltines. You will eventually not want to eat pickles, caviar, and dark chocolate . . . at the same time. And I promise—one day—you will see your toes again. Your kid's name, however, is here to stay. Her name is one of the first things anyone will know about her when they first meet, so you better put some thought into it. And it better be the right kind of thought.

Admittedly, I'm a bit of a name freak. Having four of them myself—Kristen Page Crawford Fehling—and having switched from going by my first name to going by my middle, to getting married and using every combination of all four of my names, I know how badly a jacked-up name situation can screw you. So that's the bad news. The good news is that it really is pretty simple to give your kid a decent name. I'm not saying it will be one that everyone loves, but choosing names isn't about pleasing the masses. It's about starting your child out on something at least close enough to the right foot that if he turns out to be a psychopathic serial killer weirdo it will be because you messed him up in some other area. Not because you named him Bernard.

The following are my naming do's and don'ts. Stick with them, and you will come up with something that will one day look stunning on your kid's law school diploma. Or his gas station uniform. Either way.

<u>DO</u> CONSIDER HOW IT WILL PLAY OUT ON THE PLAYGROUND. BUT NOT TOO MUCH.

It's good to at least keep in mind the fact that for the first part of your kid's life, other kids will look for ways to tease him. They just will. It's your job to not make that any easier to do. Take, for example, the (at the time) in utero daughter of my six-foot-seven, 250-pound, former NFL tight end brother. He had always liked the name "Mackenzie" for a girl. But in a moment of mental clarity in the delivery room, my brother realized that when her classmates started making trips to the golden arches, it would only be a matter of time before his little girl would be dubbed "Big Mac" for the rest of her life. It would just be too easy.

But the reason I say not to pay too much attention to this aspect is that depending on the kid, you can hedge your bets and still give a little on any possible teasing. On the flip side of my brother's case, for example, if they ever had a boy, he liked the name "Kelly." My guess is he would have been juuuuust fine.

So if you're a dweeb, and you think your kid might be a dweeb, don't name him Ernest. If you're a hippie, and you think your kid might be, oh, anything other than a hippie, don't name her Moonbeam. Or at least make her middle name "Sarah" so she has options later on. Which brings us to our next naming suggestion:

_DO_ HAVE A DAMN GOOD REASON IF YOU GO WITH A WEIRDO NAME.

Our sons' names are Crawford James and Calloway Beck. Certainly not the absolute weirdest names around. But also not exactly showing up on the "Top Ten Baby Names of the Year" list anytime soon. So allow me to make my case.

"Crawford" is my maiden name (my entire side of the family gets a shout-out: check). "James" is Jake's first name and Jake's Dad Jim's first name (father and grandfather get shout-outs: check). We call him "Ford." "Ford" comes from the end of Crawford AND is also Jake's stepdad's middle name. BAM. We just paid homage to almost all the men who somehow contributed to this gene pool with one name. Now that's what I mean by having a good reason.

Calloway is a family name on my mom's side. My uncle (Helmer Calloway), my cousin (Jonas Calloway), and my great-uncle (Kelly Calloway) all proudly carry the name. Beck is Jake's maternal grandmother's maiden name. And let's be honest: it just sounds cool. And so with this name, we have given props to pretty much anyone in the family who wasn't already included in Ford's name.

June Elizabeth is named after Jake's maternal grandmother and his mom. Jake's mom had two boys. I had had two boys. I knew the strength of that pink-ribbon desire REAL WELL. Plus I adore her, and her mom sounds like she was a badass. I figured, let's throw a little female love that way. I did feel a pang of guilt when, upon relaying the name to my Aunt Pat, she replied to my mom, "Now who are those people, and what's wrong with her own family's names?" Aunt Pat don't play. But I was so delirious from seeing a baby without a penis I probably would have let Jake name her "Frank Thomas," after all.

Simply put, in *my* book, family names are always solid. Literary favorites, significant people in your lives and even sometimes significant places can all be good "reasons" for a name. "We just liked it," is not a good reason to name your child Petunia. But if your great-aunt Petunia raised you on her own, paid for your wedding AND will be announcing next week that she just cured cancer, well, who's gonna argue with your wanting to carry on that kind of legacy?

DON'T GO WITH THE ALTERNATIVE SPELLING.

No explanation should be necessary here, but if you insist, please send my condolences to Aimee, Emileigh, Krystina, and Korie. Sincerely, Page with no 'i.'

DO THINK LIKE A SOUTHERN BELLE.

Despite living in North Carolina for almost ten years now, I still cannot fully wrap my mind around the need to inscribe every Kleenex tissue that gets near your newborn with her monogram. BUT, even those of us who may not personally choose to do so probably at least have a few Southern relatives who will bombard you with so many monogrammed gifts that you will wonder if they thought you might actually forget your kid's name if you weren't reminded of what it started with every time you changed her (monogrammed bloomer) diaper on her (monogrammed changing pad–covered) changing table eight times a day. So I do recommend at least considering what the monogram will be. You'd hate to be like Thomas Timothy Inge, Faith Taylor Allen, and Addison Samantha Somers and be stuck with monograms that read, "TIT," "FAT," and "ASS."

Now, don't they wish they'd checked in with Cousin Claire down in Savannah before signing *those* birth certificates?!

HE SAID

You know what's awesome?

Hazy IPAs. P'Zones. Fantasy football.

You know what's not awesome?

Mondays. Hand jobs. Choosing a name for your baby.

Picking names. Sounds fun, right? Wrong. Unless you like having to entertain every name under the sun. Then, right when you think you've found one that you can actually stomach, one that, up to that point, had miraculously gone unconsidered by your wife, it gets shot down faster than you can ask, "What about Jake Fehling III?"

To be fair, Page and I were essentially on the same page during the naming process. When it came to boys' names, I didn't really have any suggestions outside of "Ken Griffey Junior Fehling" (I'm a child of the nineties; what can I say). Page pitched Crawford, calling him "Ford," and Calloway, calling him "Cal." The former is a play on her maiden name and my stepdad's middle name (two family references—bonus!), and the latter is not only her uncle's name, but also an homage to baseball's "Iron Man" and some sweet golf clubs. Considering I worked in the baseball and golf industries around that time, the name played on many levels.

For the girl's name? Well, that's where it got ugly. Page had some good suggestions: Elle. Dylan. Evan. Great names. But I was thinking something . . . less *male* sounding. Something . . . older. MUCH older.

June.

It's my late maternal grandmother's name. And it's awesome.

But yeah, it's, like, nursing home old. Thus, here is where the drama came in during our first pregnancy. Ford and Cal were locks as boy options. If it was a girl? I was convinced June was it. Page was on the fence. And, because I'm a lunatic, I insisted on product testing the name everywhere we went.

There was one UNC tailgate I remember in particular, where I rounded up like ten to fifteen people, brought them in reeeeaaaaal close, then asked what they thought of the name June.

You know how when your distant uncle who never gets you presents on Christmas has to actually deliver this year because he's in town for the holidays, and his gift ends up being some lousy sweater that's, like, three sizes too big, and you have to feign excitement? That was like this . . . except they were too drunk to feign. There was no feigning. They weren't even feign-ish. They were very clear in expressing their disgust with the name.

I got defensive, stormed off, flipped a beer pong table, and headbutted a sixty-five-year-old Duke fan. Page, buoyed by the unexpected support, two-stepped the entire walk to the game. It was disgusting.

A few months later, as we neared the due date—still with no clue on the sex (we waited to find out with Ford, not so with Cal, but more on that later)—Page randomly turns to me in bed one night and says:

"I think I'm OK with 'June' if it's a girl. Yeah. I'm definitely OK with it."

"Seriously?" I reply.

"Yes. Dead serious. I also felt really sorry for you at that game—"

"YOU KNOW WHAT." *Sigh* "Very funny. I'm thrilled you've come around. And even more thrilled we're not going to give June one of the two to three boys' names you keep suggesting."

About a week later, Ford Fehling was born, and damn if that's not a money name.

Three days later, as I'm wheeling Page out of the hospital, I tell her that I'm excited to now have a girl name in the bank for our next miniature Fehling.

Silence.

Still wheeling . . . no response. Finally, after about a fifty-yard stretch of linoleum, Page stumbles through some rationale of wanting to reexamine everything for number two, taking all names into consideration again, etc., etc. Imagine the worst talk you've ever had with your boss, then multiply it by ten.

Unbelievable. We were back to the drawing board.

Fast-forward four years, another boy ("Cal": check) and about seventy-six more melodramatic tailgate debates later, and there we were again, in that same hospital, welcoming to the family a little pile of sassy flesh named . . . June.

We did it.

Well, I mean, Page delivered her, but you know what I mean.

THE NAME GAME — SHE REACTS

Jake likes to TELL you our stories. I like to USE our stories to tell you how to run your lives. I'm gonna make such a good mother-in-law one day. No, but for real. Don't name your kid something stupid.

THE NAME GAME — HE REACTS

Both of us use the word homage *in Chapter 5: check.*

So true about the Southern thing. Did you know that it's possible to embroider a rubber pacifier? Me neither. Monogrammed crib sheets, though, I think is what put me over the edge. No matter how we positioned the boys in their cribs every night, they would fall asleep face-first on the embroidery. And nothing says "preschool badass" like a toddler with his initials imprinted backwards on his forehead.

*Attempts crib escape to avoid dreaded monogram-to-face imprint.
Only makes it out of shirt.*

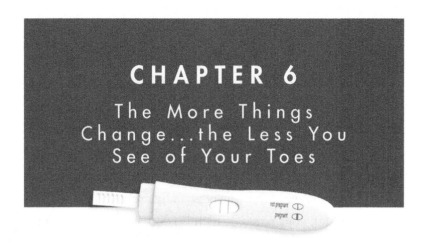

CHAPTER 6
The More Things Change...the Less You See of Your Toes

SHE SAID

Assuming you're starting this book relatively early on in your pregnancy, you may have already FELT some major body changes.

You probably haven't SEEN too many though . . . yet. Sure, you might either be always puking, on the verge of puking, or scoping out the closest trash can to see if you can make it in time for the next time you puke, but on the bright side, your boobs look amazing. So let's start there.

Your boobs. Seriously, how AMAZING are pregnant boobs?! I mean, whatever you start with up top, you're kicking it up a notch in the areas of firmness and roundness and just overall boobage. Plus, for a lot of women, your nipples do this darkening thing that makes you feel like you're some exotic-island version of yourself. AMAZING. And you know what else is amazing? Having milk drip (SURPRISE!) out of your new jugtastic island rack right in the middle of a board meeting. Oh, the glamour of early motherhood . . .

So your body is starting to change. It's gradual at first, with the bigger boobs, maybe some skin changes, and a slightly bloated tummy. Oh yeah and your boobs get bigger. But those first couple of months it's usually fairly minor and pretty gradual and for the most part you're so pumped to see some actual physical evidence of your being pregnant that you're actually excited that first time you can't button your pants. Which is good, because you can go right on ahead and say goodbye to buttons . . . and hellooooo to elastic. Lots of it.

So that's the stuff you know about. Your belly gets big when you're pregnant. Duh. So do your boobs. HALLELUJAH! But did you know that you might start to break out like a middle schooler, your skin might start to look like a patchwork quilt, and your body starts to ooze mucus from like . . . everywhere?! Mm-hmm. Yeah, you might want to start carrying around some extra tissues for your runny . . . vagina. Not what you thought I was gonna say, was it?

Get used to it, girls. Pregnancy is full of surprises, and so is your yatch. So go buy some panty liners, and get ready to wipe a couple of extra times when you pee—which you will also be doing A LOT. But hey, at least you're up a cup size or two!

Other random, inexplicable (by me) symptoms of early pregnancy include indigestion (aka *heartburn,* aka you feel like you're about to do the burp/throw-up-in-your-mouth thing like every five seconds), changes in libido (but let me just tell you, lots more blood rushing around in our bod isn't a bad thing, girls!), in-creased chance of yeast infections (aaaaaand that increased libido just got killed off), and your mouth tasting like you just bit down on a piece of metal. What the hell? I don't know. Apparently it's a thing.

But did I mention, your boobs get bigger?!

HE SAID

"Ass so fat that you could see it from the front."

—Mos Def

"Keep your eyes on my ba-bump ba-bump bump."

—Missy "Misdemeanor" Elliott

Betcha didn't know ole Mos and Missy were rapping about pregnancy in their hits, "Ms. Fat Booty" and "Work It," did ya? I'll admit, I didn't either. But it's uncanny. Give them another listen: "Sex me so good I say, 'Blah blah blah' / Work it! I need a glass of wa-tah / Boy oh boy, it's good to know ya."

Bodies, they are a-changin', my dudes. And with changing bodies comes discomfort, and with discomfort comes the need for Lycra, and there is nothing more comfortable than one big Lycra uniform.

We all have our "uniforms"—you know, the outfit we put on each night, whether it's to get ready for bed or get ready for date night. Me? If it's bedtime, you can call me Lulu Johnson. Gimme all da joggers. If we're going out, it's a pair of blue jeans and one of three buttons downs. All gingham. If Page is lucky, I add a cardigan. Mr. Rogers brings all the moms to the yard.

My uniforms may sound comfortable, but they didn't hold a candle to what Page unveiled as the preggoness set in.

"CASUAL, I'M DEFINITELY STAYING IN . . . OR AM I????" PAGE

This Page wears yoga pants. Black, stretchy yoga pants. Period.

Who knows if she was rocking these things before she got pregnant, but when I think back to Expando Page, I see yoga pants. Above the waist, it was her usual inexplicable onslaught of god-awful heavyweight cotton shirts. A 5K from 1987? Check. A comedy club shirt with the collar cut off for what I can only imagine was for a better shot at her cleavage? Yes ple—I mean, um awful. Just awful.

I learned very quickly that these suckers were going to be the new norm until the baby arrived. And every night, as much as I tried to feign disinterest in the fact that she was wearing the same pair of leggings for the twenty-second day in a row, things almost always went down like this:

[Bedroom door opens into hallway. Jake's and Page's eyes lock.]

"What?" she asks.

"Hmmm?" I reply.

"You got a problem?"

[can't . . . help . . . self]

". . . I see you're sporting those yoga pants again."

Yeah, that always ended poorly.

Three kids later, these pants should be in a museum. They've stretched, expanded, retracted, bounced back, and the only sign of wear is the fact that they now look more charcoal gray than black. If I had any money to invest, it would be in the company that makes them. In fact, I'm convinced that's why brands like Lululemon are exploding like they are—because of pregnant women. It's not because of yoga; rather, it's because they help women survive the bridge between pregnancy and *Dora the Explorer.* I know they did for us.

Speaking of charcoal gray . . .

"FINE, I'LL GO OUT, BUT DON'T THINK THAT BECAUSE I'M PREGNANT I'M NOT GONNA BE BRINGIN' THAT HEAT" PAGE

Around months four or five of our first pregnancy with Ford, Page made a trip to New York City to see some girlfriends, but the crux of the visit was so she could crush Manhattan's flagship H&M—home of one of the world's few hip maternity sections.

That's right, *H&M Maternity.* (I'm sorry, but picturing a maternity section in H&M, the home of one-size-fits-87-pound-men clothing, still slays me.)

It was on this mission to NYC that Page bought THE JEANS. A washed, faded, gray denim, with not just a gray elastic waistband, but almost a hybrid, come-halfway-up-your-torso, gray spanxband (don't bother looking; I already bought the domain).

These gray beauties made it through three pregnancies, a handful of loans to girlfriends during our "off years," and countless attempts at pregnant date nights. They were incredible, and I'm convinced H&M should spin off a separate company that sells only these jeans—for women AND men. Fellas, are you telling me that if someone made cool-looking jeans with a giant elastic/Spanx waistband, you wouldn't be all over them? I'm sorry, but I'd own every color.

God knows where those things are today, but my prayer is that some late-twenties friend of a friend of a roommate's friend is wearing them happily . . . which means there is a soon-to-be-dad out there whose life has been made a touch bit easier as well.

So, here's to you, gray, faded, Spanx-waisted, ironically merchandised H&M jeans. Thank you for making 2009 through 2014 a lot more comfortable and a hair more palatable.

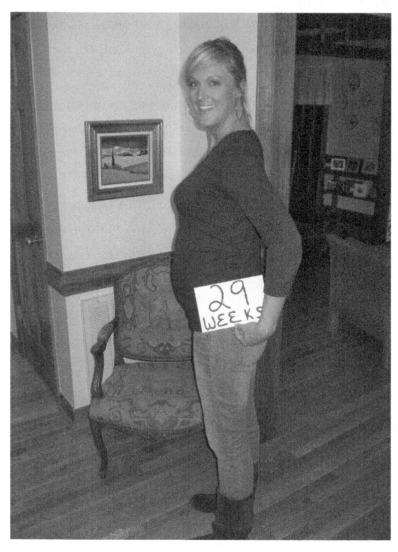

THE JEANS. Moments before they disintegrated.

THE MORE THINGS CHANGE...THE LESS YOU SEE OF YOUR TOES — SHE REACTS

So my first thought here was, "Did he forget what this chapter was about?! It's about preggo body changes, and all he's talking about is what I wore!" My second thought was, "Smartly played, Fehling." No man safely ventures into the arena of the changes to a woman's body when it comes to things expanding and makes it out alive. Unless, of course, he's talking about my third thought, which was, "I'm the only one who noticed my amazing cans?!" Huh . . .

But lastly, I have to tell you and I'm not even making a word of this up . . . as I sit here writing this reaction—and I am not even kidding right now—I have on a pair of extra-tall, black, reversible yoga pants and a navy blue Raleigh Chamber of Commerce T-shirt from at least ten years ago that has a giant hole in the armpit. I sometimes marvel at the fact that Jake has found me attractive enough on at least three occasions to even want to try to reproduce.

THE MORE THINGS CHANGE...THE LESS YOU SEE OF YOUR TOES — HE REACTS

Welp, I now have the name of my fantasy football team next season: The Jugtastic Island Racks.

So, Page, did your boobs get bigger whilst pregnant? It was unclear from your chapter. Good Lord, woman. But no, since you brought it up, I didn't really notice.

Kidding. Of course I noticed. But notice was about all I could do because you said they constantly hurt, so, yeah, my memories during this time are more yoga pants than boobs. And no, I'm not bitter.

Sigh. Back to my FANTASY team . . .

CHAPTER 7
What's Up, Doc?

SHE SAID

You love your husband, right? And you know you're gonna love your kid(s). But let me forewarn you that you are about to also fall deeply, madly, hopelessly in love with your OB-GYN too, like . . . with a quickness. In fact, you're gonna develop a pretty big crush on the entire office. It's hard not to love people when they have all the answers to something you are a complete rookie about, and they all seem equally as obsessed as you are with the biggest, coolest, most life-changing event in your life.

"Great to see you back! . . . How many weeks now?! . . . Do we know yet: boy or girl?! . . . Are you feeling OK? . . . Can I get you anything?"

It's like an attention buffet set up just for you, and you will get it from all sides. The ladies at the front desk, the assistant who leaves you the paper gown, the staff in the finance office, and, of course, the doctor. Oh, the doctor. Now, if you go to a practice like many these days, you'll likely see more than one doctor throughout your pregnancy. The idea is that since you don't ever really know when you'll go into labor, it could be anyone's turn on call, and they (ahem, *you*) don't want your water to break when your one-and-only doc is in Tahiti and your first introduction to the person birthing your child is them reaching through your spread-eagle legs, trying to shake your hand in between pushes. So you meet them all, and you love them all, and you start to feel like one great big polygamist family. Especially when your husband, your doctor, and you are all in one room together and you are being violated with what they claim is a "sonogram instrument."

Yep.

This is on your first "real" pregnancy appointment, where they're basically looking to confirm that you're pregnant, determine how far along you are, and make sure that things look like they're on the right track. But the baby is so small at this point (around eight to nine weeks) that they can't do what you typically see in movies when they show sonograms (goop on your belly, cord attached to a paddle thingy rubbing along the outside of your tummy, heartbeat sounds in the background, the doc asks if you're ready to start shopping for baseball gloves, you cry happy tears). Yeah, no. This is not that. This feels more like some *Da Vinci Code* ritualistic group-sex experiment. Darkened room, soft whirring in the background, you lie on a table, "comforted" by your husband holding your hand while essentially a perfect stranger (albeit a stranger you have an inexplicably strong obsession with, but still . . .) shoves a giant penis-shaped piece of plastic up your hoo-ha. Most disturbing part for me? The condom. Because that means that the giant penis-shaped piece of plastic has been in about seventeen other hoo-has that same day. No, thank you.

But from then on, don't worry—the doctor appointments are pretty straightforward. Arrive, pee in a cup, weight check, heartbeat check, pat on the ass, send you on your way. There's one where you chug something that tastes like expired Orange Crush (gestational diabetes check), and some where you start doing fun stuff like insurance paperwork and things, but the middle-of-pregnancy appointments are, for the most part, all fully clothed and, frankly . . . almost boring.

Fast-forward to the end of your third trimester and your "progress checks." You're back. You're naked from the waist down. You're in stirrups. And they're all up in your vag again. Only this time, it's not with the sonogram dildo. This time, they just use their fingers. It's like making out with your high school boyfriend while your husband watches.

Totally normal.

HE SAID

Aaaaaaaaaand we're live from your wife's vagina!!

Yep. Welcome to pregnancy doctor visits. Chicks, dudes, janitors, strangers, young children, everyone, it seems, had their hands in Page's crotch over the course of those twenty-seven months.

It's such a bizarre feeling, OB appointments. I mean, I'm not the jealous type, but there is something unnatural about the process the first time through. Prior to Page carrying Ford, the only twinge of jealousy I can remember is while dating, when she told me she "studied" with the basketball team while at UNC. Right. But you know what, it's cool. I once tried out for JV at Carolina. I dunked, like, once in a game. Vince Carter? Overrated. Antawn Jamison? A bum. But anyway, where was I? Oh that's right. The OB. I would have to psyche myself up to be there:

Jake, another dude, people, an entire village of humans is about to feel around in Page's nether region. Everything is on the up and up. Just let it happen. Just let it . . .

. . . Is that a fifteen-inch dildo? WTF, doc? What even is that thing? What exactly are you checking in this appointment—Page's rib cage? Could you not have gone with a smaller device? What about that one over there? It looks completely sturdy, perfectly sized, wonderfully average—what's that? That's your pen? Ah, of course. No, totally. It was way too small to do the trick anyway . . . um . . . moving on . . .

Seriously, though, it's weird. Once I got past the Ron Jeremy of OB devices, I then had to deal with the MALE doctor diving right in. Now, I'm sure this process was no picnic for Page either, and if it was, then we are officially never picnicking again as a family, but still, imagine if the tables were turned:

"Page, could you please join me for my annual physical this morning? Most of the checks will be done by a decidedly unattractive man, except for one small part. The testicle check will be done by a highly educated and attainably hot female. I'm going to need you to sit directly next to me during the entire procedure, while not looking too awkward as you try to cast your gaze upon anything in the room except my groin."

Which leads to my closing remarks. A plea to all expectant fathers, really. Guys. GUYS. Please choose your seat wisely during these appointments. Page and I tried to schedule appointments around lunch, so we could attend together, then, if there was time, head out for a picnic. Er, head out for a bite to eat. With that in mind, I always seemed to be just ending a phone call or meeting beforehand, so when I arrived, I would inevitably come tearing into the OB's office and mumble something hurriedly about needing to find Page. After navigating the office labyrinth, I'd somehow ultimately end up in Page's room mere seconds before, um, entry.

On what was easily the most memorable of those fire drills, I burst into a room filled with not only Page and her OB, but also two additional nurses. I can't for the life of me remember why all the excitement, but I'm sure Page will gently remind me in her reaction below. There were people standing, sitting, kneeling, burpeeing, everything. I quickly scan for and find the lone open seat in the room and park myself there, under the disapproving stares of the thirty-seven spectators. *Sorry, gang, I'm nine seconds late for the most awkward hour of my week. My bad.*

It didn't take long for me to discover why that seat was still open. After I get myself situated and silence my phone, I look up and am exactly six inches from Page's vagina. And before I could say "Uh, Page . . .?" the doc swoops in and asks Page to put her feet in the stirrups. She doesn't blink and slams those size 11s in there as if it was the Kentucky Derby. I freeze. The doc instantly realizes what she's done. The room goes silent. Page is still clueless as to what is happening. Granted, I have now had far more graphic views of Page's baby-making parts, but at the time, this was . . . this was . . . well . . .

One of the nurses said it best. Seeing my mouth agape, she smiled, intercepted my stare, and said the only two words that could have added the necessary levity to the situation:

"MERRY CHRISTMAS!"

WHAT'S UP, DOC? — SHE REACTS

Oh, the "Merry Christmas" visit . . .

Yep. That was a good one. Made better only by the fact that after that comment, we all started laughing so hard that if I'd had pants on, I would have peed in them. If you'll recall though . . . no pants. Only stirrups. And Jake's face, I believe, was it . . . six inches?! Did he say?! From my vagina?! While I laughed so hard I PEED?! (Which A., isn't hard to do when you're pregnant. And B., whatever.) That's what you get for being late to appointments.

A little pee in the face never killed anybody.

WHAT'S UP, DOC? — HE REACTS

Thrilled to hear you thought it was as awkward as I did. Worst. Christmas. Ever. Coal in my stocking would have been preferred. Sing it with me, kids: "Jakey, the red-faced husband, had a very shiny . . . wife's vagina. And if you ever saw it, you would even say—" OK, I'll stop.

Truly, though, what an odd situation those visits were, and it's all only compounded by the fact that they became, as you said, normal.

Jake *calm, legs crossed*: "So, doc, how is your family?"

Doc *calm, all up in Page's crotch*: "Wonderful, thank you for asking."

Jake: "Ah, I see you're going with the Baby's Arm 4,000 today. I just saw it earned FDA approval. Excellent choice, doc."

Doc: "It is indeed. I can do about thirty of these a day with this thing and never get tired. Can I offer you a Fresca?"

Page: "Make it two."

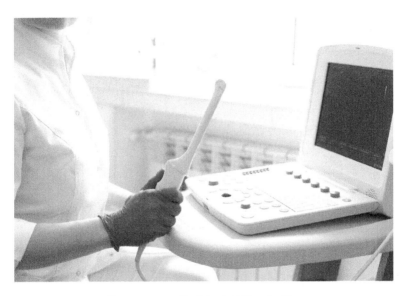

Sex toy or medical device? You decide.

CHAPTER 8
The Preggo Police

SHE SAID

One of Jake's grandmothers had seven children. SEVEN. EFFING. CHILDREN. That means she was pregnant for almost six years. SIX. EFFING. YEARS. I never got to meet her because she died while Jake was still in middle school, but I've always liked her anyway. You know why? Because from the stories I've heard, whenever someone used to ask her how she did it, with all those pregnancies and all those kids, she would always respond, "Do you think I ever would have had seven kids if I had had to be sober through all those pregnancies?!" Point well made, Mimi. And cheers to you!

But my, how times have changed.

Back in the early fifties and sixties, when our grandmothers were knocked up, they were blissfully unaware of the harmful effects of things like alcohol, cigarettes, and Molly. Now, while I'm certainly not advocating we all light up over dirty martinis in the delivery room, I think things these days have gone a little too far.

When I first found out I was pregnant, I was surprised by the extensive list of don'ts coming from my doctor's office. There are certain things you know you'll forego upon finding yourself with child, but there are other things that come out of left field. Plane travel, for example, probably isn't a great idea when you can no longer see your feet (or those of the person in front of you). Contact sports are put on hold until after delivery. Keg stands become a thing of the past faster than you can do a handstand and count to ten. But did you know enjoying a turkey sub is outside the realm of preggo possibility too? And that you can't sleep on your back after week twenty? Well, there are plenty of people out there who do know these handy facts. And they're only too happy to fill you in if you're caught in the act of breaking any of the "rules." I like to call these people the Preggo Police.

Frustratingly enough (but not all that surprisingly), officers of the Preggo Police squad are usually male. Which, since they'll never have to follow their own instructions, makes them all the more douchey. The saying, *"People who live in glass houses shouldn't throw stones,"* comes to mind. Only in this case it would be more like, *"People who are still allowed to eat sushi can take that sushi and shove it up their ass."*

My first encounter with the Preggo Police happened one day early on in my first preggo-ness when I ordered a soda at lunch. I'd barely gotten the fourth syllable of "Diet Pepsi" out when I incurred the wrath of Officer Caffeine.

"You know, you really should have juice or even water instead. Did you know too much caffeine has been proven to cause miscarriages in the first trimester?"

Why no, oh Genius One, somehow I must have missed that little tidbit in the dozen What to Expect When You're Expecting-*style books I've read already. So I guess you're saying the heroin I experimented with last week probably wasn't a good idea either?*

Let's get a little something straight: I've already given up lunch meat, alcohol, sushi, any worth-a-damn amount of tuna fish, highlights in my hair, sleeping on my back, sleeping on my stomach, sleeping much at all, cold and flu medications, a pain-free back, any prayer of fitting into something with the word small—or, let's be honest, even medium—on the tag, strenuous exercise (ok, so there are some perks), my bra size (again . . . not all preggo "sacrifices" are that bad), my shoe size (but then there's that), my right to not have perfect strangers grope my mid-section, and the list goes on and on. Allow me this one little liquid pleasure sans judgment, won't you?

My best advice here, girls? Everything in moderation . . . including well-meaning "advice" from otherwise would-be a-holes. And if you just can't take it anymore, go find a grandma to talk to. She'll pour you a cold one and tell you that *you're* the real a-hole for listening to those idiots.

Mimi's brood. Deserving of at LEAST one martini per child.

HE SAID

Let me begin by saying you Preggo Police are the worst. THE worst.

OK, with that out of the way, I can safely, calmly, reasonably move forward here without—you know what? I tried. Have I mentioned that you're the worst? As my boy Pac would say, die slow.

OK, that was a touch dramatic. But I chose those lyrics purposefully—it's the Preggo Police that make an already impossible nine to ten months feel like a slow death. Just let my wife and me freak out in peace, thank you very much.

There are three types of you jackasses out there, and since we've already started to run with the police analogy, we'll stay with it. I've seen *The Wire;* I've got this.

OFFICER

You're new to the force. You had a kid, like, nine minutes ago, so of course you know exactly what you're talking about. It's OK, we get it—you're excited. You made it out of the academy and have been around the block. Your method of delivery is almost exclusively via passive aggression.

"Oh, wow, I didn't know Walmart made generic prenatal vitamins. Nice. I'm sure they're great."

Or, how about this classic:

"When did you say that flight was again? Ah. And your due date, when was that again?" *pauses, counts fingers* *"No, totally. I'm sure everything will be fine."*

Thanks, Officer. Am I free to go?

LIEUTENANT

Douches reporting for duty! Lieutenants have multiple kids, they're salty as hell, and they've done their homework on the case at hand. You could even say they've STUDIED all angles of the pregnancy process.

"Hey, Jake, how're ya holdin' up?"

"My boobs are killing me." *cackle like hyenas, fist pound* *"But no, we're good man, thanks."*

"And Page? Feeling OK?"

"She's great, just moving a little slower these days."

"Oh . . . well . . . that's good that she's moving, because . . . actually, this is a coincidence, I just read something that says stud—"

"Dude, are you about to say 'studies show'?"

"Yeah, because studies show that steady, light exercise during pregnancy helps fend off allergies, autism, AIDS, and . . ."

You get the point.

CHIEF

One guess here, ladies and gentlemen? Bingo. These are your parents and in-laws. And even though the Chief has seen and done it all, offers super-helpful commonsense advice, and you respect the shit out him/her, their comments are easily the most annoying.

"Sweetie . . . and I don't mean to pry . . . but were you planning on covering this hole in the drywall in the nursery before the baby comes—"

"OF COURSE I KNOW THERE'S A HOLE IN THE WALL AND STINKBUGS ARE FLYING OUT OF IT AND YES I KICKED THAT HOLE IN MYSELF WHEN I COULDN'T FIGURE OUT HOW TO PUT THE CRIB TOGETHER AND OMG WHY DO YOU SAY THE MOST OBVIOUS STUFF DUHHHHHHHAAAAHHHHHHH!!!!"

"OK . . . because it's just that if one of those bugs bit the baby . . ."

--

And—spoiler alert—GREAT NEWS! These esteemed members of the force will follow you around post-baby as well! As your kids grow older, the comments will evolve into, "Miss Anderson is the worst teacher in the school. Also, she has a lazy eye. Everyone knows that. You'd better hope June lands Miss Carter instead." Uh, yeah, no shit. EVERYONE knows about Miss Anderson, except . . . who's Miss Anderson again?

So, to all of you smarter-than-Siri, a-hole Preggo Police out there, please, I implore you: keep your #studies and #research to yourselves.

Calls school to request Miss Carter

THE PREGGO POLICE — SHE REACTS

You've seen The Wire? HA! That one got me. Loved the officer breakdown. And for anyone still scratching their head, his "boy Pac" refers to rapper Tupac Shakur. Because in another life, Jake wishes he could have been a nineties hip-hop artist. And I would have GLADLY been his back-up dancer. Also, good call on the people who've just had a few kids and think they have a license to give everyone else advice. What a bunch of jerks. Next thing you know, they'll be writing a book on pregnancy like they know something!

THE PREGGO POLICE — HE REACTS

So Mimi and Molly walk into a bar . . .

I forgot about the Dude Preggo Police. Yeah, so maybe they're the worst. Please tell me I'm not like that. Please. Every time we're with friends and the guy speaks up about his wife's pregnancy, I want to deck him.

But . . . sigh . . . I don't know, actually . . . sometimes they have a point. A buddy once cautioned me that the third shot of tequila you had that one time was probably a bad idea, and we should at least consider that it led to Cal's gravelly voice . . .

Sleeps on couch

SECOND TRIMESTER

Wait, Is This Really Happening?

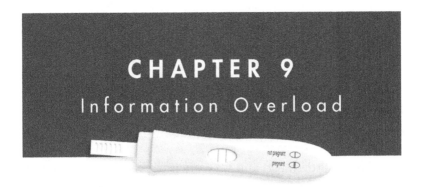

CHAPTER 9
Information Overload

SHE SAID

When I actually get my ish together and have the time to get ready for something (like, say, a big interview for work), I am an over-preparer. I read far too many articles. I make far too many notes. I come up with more questions than I could ever hope to ask in an hour-long special, let alone a three-minute segment on a morning newscast.

I'm also THE biggest procrastinator on the entire planet.

And when I combine extreme procrastination with my penchant for over-preparedness, it can lead to a pretty shitty hour and a half before whatever it is that I'm preparing for.

Reading.

Taking notes.

Rereading.

Changing notes.

Making lists.

Printing every piece of information I can find.

Cursing the m-effing printer for not working because doesn't it know I'M IN A HURRY, DAMMIT. I only have an hour and a half and I can't wait for your toner issues!!

It's all a little much and very often backfires on me when I end up using ZERO of the information I prepared and instead just ask the mayor to play the popular party game Catch Phrase with me on TV. Because—not that it speaks well of us as a society or me as a journalist—I know most people would rather watch that than hear about the economic impact of the new downtown revitalization anyway.

Sigh.

So please know and understand that it is from a place of "I get it" that I come to you and beg you to STOP READING EVERY BABY ARTICLE YOU SEE ON FACEBOOK. And for the love of God, please stop reposting them. It will not help you. It will make you crazy. And it will make all of your sane friends unfriend you. Speaking of friends . . .

As we've mentioned in previous chapters, Jake and I were some of the first of our friends to reproduce. That led to the unfortunate happenstance of us becoming go-tos for baby, pregnancy, and newborn questions.

Bad idea.

We are dumb-dumbs.

We didn't know anything more than they did. The only difference was that we'd done it before with one (then two, now—WTF—*three!*) mini humans before they did. All that we could offer were some "here's what sort of worked for us" pieces of advice and a story about how poorly we handled the situation so they could laugh at us and learn from our mistakes.

Now THOSE are the kinds of articles that are worth a damn to read. And *those* are the kinds of friends worth having. So I guess that's my point: everyone should be just like us.

Wait that's not it.

My point is actually this: even though pregnancy and mayors are vastly different, the same Catch Phrase principle applies (I just made that up). Over-preparing will do you no good. It will only make you stressed and sweaty, and when shit hits the fan, all you're gonna do is drop back and punt anyway, so you might as well just cover the basics and hope for the . . .

beep . . . beep . . . beep

Rhymes with "rest" . . .

BEEP . . . BEEP . . . BEEP

Opposite of "worst" . . .

BEEP . . . BEEP . . . BEEEEEEEEP!

BEST! Hope for the best!

Congrats! You . . . win?

HE SAID

AIRHORN NOISES

Welcome to the second trimester!!!

AIRHORN NOISES

Betcha didn't think you'd make it, did you, fellas? Well, you're here, and now you're in the homestretch. Things are getting real at this point.

As in, really real. Like, "Excuse me, WTF is happening to my wife's body" real.

Well, fortunately, between Chapter 8's Preggo Police and the one billion books out there, you're never too far from advice. Ah, books. Did you know people still read books? When we told people Page was pregnant, she and I were showered with books. Real. Life. *Books.* As in, like, made from paper. Weird, right?

Now, there are far more books out there for women, so again, this is more of a Page problem, but I definitely had more than one conversation like this with a couple buddies of mine:

"How's Page doing?"

"Great! How's your wife?"

"OK, eeeeasy. I mean, are you guys handling the pregnancy thing well?"

"Yeah, I think . . . well, yeah, it's going as well, it . . . yes."

"'Cause there's this one book I read that—"

"Yep, I'm out."

Which leads me to one of the main drivers behind me and Page writing this train wreck: While the notion that "there is nothing out there for soon-to-be dads" is completely false, whiny, and blown out of proportion, a claim that "there is nothing _good_ out there for soon-to-be dads" is valid.

In no way do I think that we're here to fill that void completely, but there is a pretty shocking amount of stuff out there that is just plain bad. These books either make you feel like shit, or they make you want to stab the book and/or author right in the spine. Look, we're not cavemen. We're open to advice, but it has to be delivered effectively. For example, here are a few dos and don'ts for pregnancy books for dads (which I fully realize is the single most hypocritical thing you'll read today):

DO keep it real. We care and we swear. We aren't complete douchebags, so don't paint us that way, and going through a pregnancy—especially for the woman—is shitty, so let's not edit out the, well, shit, shall we? And yes, I meant that literally and figuratively. More on that in the delivery chapter . . .

DON'T keep it _TOO_ real. Any time a book gets too, um, informative, I either tune out, or I get grossed out. Oh, really, I should expect more discharge from my wife? Sweet. And while we're here, can we please talk about how _discharge_ is one of the more low-key completely horrible words out there? _Moist_ gets all the headlines, but _discharge_ is pretty freaking awful.

DO give us some credit. We're not complete idiots. Dad stereotypes are so tired, it's a joke. Look, we're still guys, but we're not hopeless. I obviously know that it was a stork with a hat that put the baby in my wife's belly. I've seen *Dumbo*. Duh.

DON'T give us *TOO* much credit. I've never been pregnant *OR* been this close to someone who is. How am I supposed to know that morning sickness goes away after three months, so I shouldn't blame your salty attitude on that in month seven? Bueller...?

Those are a couple of good starting points. I'm all for more information, but please make it palatable. You know, like the exact opposite of discharge.

vomits

INFORMATION OVERLOAD — SHE REACTS

Jake, I think you actually have information underload . . . because morning sickness does NOT stop after three months. For SOME women it does (or, at least, it gets significantly better). For SOME women it lasts so long and is so bad that you have to take medicine that keeps you from wanting to puke, but makes you not poop for like a month. Pick your poison. And while we're at it, morning sickness can happen anytime. Not just in the morning . . . and definitely anytime someone says "discharge."

INFORMATION OVERLOAD — HE REACTS

Weird, I had no idea you were a procrastinator. We only started writing this book in 2010 . . .

I agree with you, though; there is so much content out there to digest. It's only been ten years, but I can't imagine being pregnant with the way social media is today. Especially with Alexa and our devices listening to everything we say. Can you imagine what Instagram ad I'm about to have served up with all of this discharge talk?

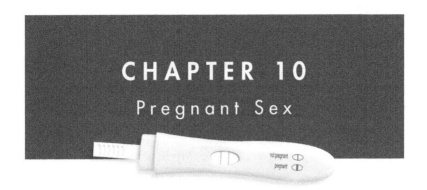

CHAPTER 10

Pregnant Sex

SHE SAID

Oh . . . Oh . . . OHMYGODGIRLSYOUAREGONNALOVEPREG-NANTSEEEEEEEXXXXXX

Ahem.

Excuse me.

Where was I?

Ah, yes. Sex. When you're pregnant. Is AMAZING.

You are curvy and swollen and somehow firmer than you've ever been, all at the same time. Your blood is pumping faster and there's more of it and it's going to all the right places. Like riiiiight there . . . no, just over a little teeny bit . . . yeah, there . . . there . . . OHMYGODYESRIGHTTHEEEEEEERRRRRRREEEEE.

What was I saying? Lost my train of thought for a sec . . .

Oh yeah, the sex. When you're pregnant. Is AMAZING.

I do remember reading some scientific reason behind the whole extra-blood thing (and yes, it was in one of those books I told you not to read), but really, who cares WHY?! For once in your life, you are able to have sex with wild abandon. If you were trying to get pregnant before, then mission accomplished! Now you can get back to doing it just for fun. And if you had an ooops pregnancy then . . . welp . . . too late. Might as well enjoy what got you into this mess!

Oh, and your body. Your BAH-DEE. Flat-chested women, you are suddenly Pamela Anderson. Chubby women, you are suddenly solid in places that usually wiggle and jiggle. Skinny women, you suddenly have curves . . . because we all feel really sorry for you that not enough curves used to be your biggest body issue. But I digress.

Where was I? Right. The sex. When you're pregnant. And how AMAZING it is.

Pregnant sex is truly a win-win for everyone. You've got your eyes on the prize, which is suddenly so much easier to, errr . . . win. And he's got his eyes on . . . your boobs. Which, much like the overall sex right now . . . are AMAZING.

One minor caveat with the boobs though, boys . . . you can look but you canNOT touch. You just let those giant orbs float and flounce and lure you in right at the tip of your nose, but DON'T YOU DARE let the tip of your nose (or the tip of anything else, for that matter) touch them because they are so effing painful and sensitive to the touch that—wait a minute . . .

Speaking of sensitive to the touch . . .

Yep, pretty sensitive to the touch right . . . yep . . . right . . .

THERE . . . OHMYGODYESRIGHTTHEREAGAAAAAI-
IIIIIINNNNNN!!!!!

HE SAID

Nope. You're not suckering me into this.

Boobs.

Jake . . . just, *no.* Don't do it. Everyone in your family is going to read this book.

BEWBS.

Welp, here we are. Chapter 10. Pregnant Sex. Let's get it over with. What a fun topic to write about when you know this book is going to serve as a baby shower gift for every pregnant relative and close family friend who has known you since birth.

But you know what? Screw it. And yes, I guess I do mean that literally.

Pregnant sex is legit, y'all.

Although, I guess if we're being honest with ourselves, it's probably not the sex that's legit (I'm no Peter North, as Page can attest), it's just that . . . damn if a pregnant woman's body isn't hot as hell.

Boobs: larger. Curves: accentuated. Boobs: larger. You get the point. I don't know, fellas . . . it just did it for me. Page? Well, she obliged. That's probably all I can say. And God bless her. Could you imagine weighing one hundred pounds more and wanting to do it more often? Wait—don't answer that.

I remember reading my first pregnancy book, and when I hit this chapter, I got totally skeeved out. The author (a man) had zero sense of humor and described his lust for the pregnant female body in a *WAY* too serious manner. His writing had me throwing up in my mouth:

> "Perhaps it was the increased diameter of her areolas, or the flourish of her pubis region, but I found myself in a near permanent state of erection. It was a sensation I welcomed, and I urged her to submit to my missionary prowess at a significantly increased rate as compared to our typical weekly average . . ."

Just gross.

But also KINDA dead on (minus the flourish). I mean, I was always down to get down, but adding the extra skin, weight, and curves—and I'm talking about me too, gang; I put on the freshman forty with our first kid—added a level of sloppiness. A level of difficulty. A level of weird. I was James Bond meets Shaun White meets Ron Jeremy, and my weapon of choice was the extended back tickle turned boob graze turned thigh rub. I was the master of not-so-subtle hints. I'd like to think it was an irresistible move, one to which Page consistently fell prey, but in reality, she was typically still bloated off a burrito from earlier that night and just wanted to speed up the inevitable.

"Page . . . are you awake? . . . Page? . . . PAGE!?"

"Hmmmfrhghghgmmm?"

"Sorry, did I wake you? Anyway, I noticed you're pregnant and your boobs are bigger. Wanna do it?"

"You said that last night . . . and the night before . . . and . . ."

"Shhhhhhh . . ." *starts tickling Page's sideboob*

Fatality. Pregnant sex wins.

PREGNANT SEX — SHE REACTS

Welp, I am officially blushing. And going on a diet. One hundred pounds?! And what even was that paragraph. Was that real? A "permanent state of erection" sounds pretty terrible. Please God, don't let our families read this chapter.

Also, I don't know who Peter North is, but I'm guessing I shouldn't Google his name on my work computer to find out?

PREGNANT SEX — HE REACTS

Look, we couldn't write a pregnancy book without a sex chapter. It's part of the process. And you should always trust the process. Even when the process involves your wife telling you to write a book about pregnancies and a chapter about sex. Yeah, you should totally trust that process.

I'm glad to hear you enjoyed that time period as much as I did though. Unless . . . wait . . . did you just accomplish the first multiple fake O in literary history???

CHAPTER 11
Pregnant Social Life

SHE SAID

About halfway into your pregnancy is when you start to realize how cute going-out clothes are. And that none of them fit you. You feel like a beached whale, and who wants to go out anyway because you've started to realize that everyone in your life is a degenerate alcoholic, and they all want you to drive their drunken asses around town.

Jake is the worst at this. Jake, I love you, but YOU ARE THE WORST AT THIS.

During my first pregnancy I tried so hard to be the cool, good-sport pregnant chick who stayed out late and voluntarily carted hoards of drunkies around from place to place. I mean, "I literally can't drink anyway, so I might as well save you a few bucks AND help you get home safely too!" Read: when you (or your wife, depending upon the gender of said drunkie) get knocked up, you owe me big time. I still have like seven million of these favors to cash in.

There are so many only-sober-one nights I can think back on that it's hard to pick a favorite. There was the time I got so fed up with Jake's critiques of my driving that even though we were following another car to location two of our double date with them, I pulled over to the side of the road and threatened to sit there until he sobered up and could drive us home himself. Or the time when it was three in the morning, and I was doing drop-offs after the post-club Waffle House run while about to pee in my pants, and the entire car started chanting, "Boo, Page!" when I asked if we could go straight home instead of circling the block for one more round of the "Call Me Maybe" car dance. But one night in particular comes to mind when I think about how awesome it is to be the DD for forty weeks.

So Jake and I get home. It's like two in the morning. He is in rare form. I'm about thirty-seven weeks pregnant and just haven't been feeling great all day: little queasy, little headachy. Oh, and THIRTY-SEVEN WEEKS EFFING PREGNANT, so not entirely at my peak. We go to our room to get ready for bed and before I'm even halfway through brushing my teeth, Jake is already passed out face up on top of our covers snoring like a buzzsaw. So loudly. SO. SO. LOUDLY. I somehow find a way to both protect my eardrums and finish up my evening routine, get in bed . . . and start to feel nauseous in like, ten seconds. I half-heartedly ask Jake if he'll get up and bring me a trashcan to put by the bed in case I need to throw up during the night. He sort of snorts and rubs his face and continues on his wildly attractive snoring rant. I get up to get it myself and before I make it back to the lying-down position I start to feel my dinner come up. In no time I'm perched on the side of the bed, emptying everything in my stomach into the mini plastic bathroom trash can. In between wretches I notice the snoring has stopped. Is he awake? Did he just roll over and go back to sleep quietly? Then I feel a warm hand on my lower back. He's awake! He's rubbing my back and prolly gonna reach up to pull my hair back off my face me in a second. *See! He's not just being drunk and inconsiderate and taking advantage of a built-in DD!* Then the pressure of the hand gets a little harder. And harder. I'm in denial. *This is not happening. Yes it is. HE IS TRYING TO NUDGE MY THIRTY-SEVEN-WEEKS-PREGNANT ASS OFF THE BED.* And then, I shit you not, these words actually come out of his mouth: "Hey babe can you go do that in the bathroom? It grosses me out when people puke in front of me."

I wanted to take that little plastic trash can and empty its contents onto his head. But you know what I did instead? Made him stand at my feet during childbirth. And he thought a little puke made him sick to his stomach?! Ahhhh sweet revenge.

HE SAID

I'm willing to bet the house that Page said I was the least-sympathetic pregnant husband ever. Well, I'm sorry that I like to have fun. I'm sorry that I'm a good time, Page. I'm sorry that I like to drink beer and dance. I'm sorry that you feel bloated, Page. I feel fantastic, and our lives are about to end, so . . . you're damn right I'm gonna do the Wobble.

In retrospect, I definitely could have/should have downshifted. It probably wasn't fun for Page to watch me sloppily bring the house down with an amazing freestyle session at my ten-year high school reunion ("Ayyyyye, I'm the presidente . . . I like my pasta . . . um . . . al dente!"—WTF), or destroy some five-year-old on a reception dance floor at a buddy's wedding, or vomit after both of these magical moments. Actually, she probably loved that last one.

Looking back, if I could offer one piece of advice for the dudes reading this book, fellas, I know this feels like you won the lottery, but . . .

BE CAREFUL HOW OFTEN YOU PULL THE DD CARD.

I wore that thing out. You see, when you're pregnant with your first child, you're still sort of in let's-go-out-every-weekend mode, so, hell yeah, Page, I'd love for you to drive to what is really an inconsequential BBQ at a fringe friend's house. When you're pregnant with your second, your social life is definitely curbed, but, sure, Page, I'd love it if I could drink while you haul me around town on the one night this quarter that I'm gonna turn up . . . and in all likelihood, throw up. By the time you're on your third (or fourth or fifth . . . okay I'm stopping there) pregnancy, you've finally started figuring out that all of these DD requests have been piling up like IOUs in *Dumb and Dumber* . . . which is a very fitting metaphor.

As it currently stands, I'm never going to be able to do any of this ever again without serving as the driver. If there is anything even remotely resembling a social gathering for Page and me to attend, we are getting a sitter, I'm behind the wheel, and wifey is gettin' lit. It's that simple.

Or, you can just Uber everywhere and thoroughly piss your baby momma off over the fact that you've rendered her revenge card useless. I play the game a bit. Uber sometimes, DD others. Make it seem like you're paying her back, because there's going to be a night sometime soon when your boys are in town and Uber is surging 4.5 times, and you need to call in your boo from the bullpen. That's right, you want the righty—the sober one with a mean 65 mph cruise control and a salty disposition. She'll get you out of that jam.

But now we've come full circle. You owe her in this scenario, too. You know what? Just lock your doors when your wife is pregnant. Hide yo kids, hide yo (pregnant) wife. Just ride out those nine months so you can ride out to that next BBQ in style . . . sitting shotgun.

PREGNANT SOCIAL LIFE — SHE REACTS

I am getting re-pissed off just reading this. I hope you've enjoyed the $7 million we've spent on Uber this past year because your ass is driving us EVERYWHERE between now and 2035. And you rhymed, "I'm your Presidente" with, "You like your pasta al dente" at the reunion. NOT an amazing freestyle session. But the five-year-old dance floor takedown? Now THAT was some good shit.

PREGNANT SOCIAL LIFE — HE REACTS

This reminded me of the time when, as a ten-year-old kid, I watched in horror as my brother threw up after trying to eat a tomato. I can't handle seeing people throw up, so I lost my lunch right there and then, too. I shit you not, our dog and cat witnessed the carnage and followed suit. Four living, breathing, puking people/animals in one kitchen.

All of that to say, Vomitphobia is real, and those inflicted stand as some of society's most empathetic figures. Page, maybe someday you can understand my plight. And drive me to my next doctor's appointment. While I drink.

P.S. You snore too.

CHAPTER 12
Pink or Blue? Or Green or Yellow?

SHE SAID

I know, I know . . . you don't care what you're having. Boy or girl, you just want a healthy baby. We all said it.

We all heard it.

We all lied.

Both you and your husband SO care whether or not your baby is a boy or a girl. And so does everyone else in your life.

There are a select few who say they only want one or the other. They are lying, not only to the rest of us, but also to themselves. They are typically either men who claim, "If God gives me only daughters, he's getting back at me for how I treated women my whole life." (Eeeeeasy, player. You wish you had that much bad behavior to look back on.) Or women who claim that they want only boys because, "Boys are so much easier than girls."

Both of these people are stupid.

A house full of only girls (and let's be honest, even with just two, that house is full) might mean some more tantrums and drama and "I hate you!!"s during those teen years, but guess what? When everyone is married off and planning holidays and get-togethers and family vacations and, well, life, guess which side gets first dibs. The wives. Your girls. Remind yourself of that when you're sitting third row at your seventeenth Taylor Swift concert this year.

A house full of boys, meanwhile, is most certainly also a full house. And everything in it is broken. You are the loudest family anywhere you go. You have wrestling matches to "calm down" for bedtime. And everything in your life involves a superpower, a superhero costume, and superhero underpants with the most god-awful skid marks you've ever seen. But you get those sweet baby-boy and little-boy years when YOU are the biggest superhero in his life, and if you play your cards right maybe he'll marry an only child so you actually get to see him on an actual Christmas Day past the age of twenty-five.

But let's be real. Most people want both. At some point . . . after some indeterminate amount of "trying" for whatever sex has yet to come forth . . . most couples are going for both a boy and a girl. Why do you think you see so many families with two, three, FOUR (?!!!) boys or girls in a row and then they (FINALLY!) get the opposite sex and then NO. MORE. CHILDREN. Very seldom do you see a family with three boys, then a girl, and then . . . oh, one more boy tacked on to the end for good measure. Nope. Why gamble with fate? Case in point: our Junebug. As one of my best friends put it, a girl after two boys is like God's little exclamation

point—as in, a very happy ending. And as in . . . very much an
ENDING.

So then the real question with each pregnancy becomes—
should you find out what you're having beforehand? The short
answer? No. The long answer? Yes. If you're Jake. And if you're
wrong. Which you are if you say you should find out what sex
you're having beforehand.

Look. I get it. You're a planner. You want to decorate the nursery. You want to buy clothes. You want to feel more bonded to the
baby. Crap, crap, and more crap. If you go too gender-specific the
first go-round, then you're totally screwed if you want to reuse
baby gear for an opposite-sex number two. If you know what
you're having before your baby shower(s), PEOPLE WILL GET
YOU NOTHING BUT CLOTHES. They will be adorable. People
simply will not be able to resist outfitting your little one with useless, spectacularly precious one-time-wear attire. You will want
to die at the cuteness. You will also want to die at the price tag of
buying your own car seat. But no one likes to buy too many yellow
and green onesies. So if people don't know what you're having they
will get you the stuff you actually need—the stuff you can use for
multiple babies. Just for fun, go see what a hospital-grade breast
pump is going for these days. Mm-hmm. And let me let you in
on a little secret: you will get those clothes anyway. If you don't
know what sex the baby is ahead of time, people lose their damn
minds when that baby arrives. And apparently, they go to find
them at Baby Gap.

First baby?

"OMG, he/she is finally here!! And we finally know it's a boy/girl! Get him/her out of that green/yellow and into this three-piece seersucker onesie/pastel flamingo Lilly Pulitzer romper!" (Can you tell we had babies in the South?)

First of one sex after one or more of the opposite sex?

Forget it. Let the floodgates open as excitement pours into his or her closet.

Second boy or girl after already having one of the same?

Wamp waaamp. It's hand-me-down central. But at least SOMEONE will wear that six-month–sized Baby Burberry peacoat again!

But that's just the superficial stuff. What really matters is the surprise. And I do mean SURPRISE. Couples who find out ahead of time love to say, "It's a surprise no matter when you find out." Those couples are wrong. They just are. Looking at an ultrasound or having a doctor tell you what your baby is or even (squeal!) biting into a cupcake and seeing one or the other color of food dye in there is just not the same as having forty (-plus?!) weeks of wondering what's in there . . . pushing for God knows how long (still no clue) . . . finally seeing a head start to come out (still no clue) . . . then shoulders (still no clue) . . . then a chest . . . and tummy . . . and . . . HOLY SHIT IT'S A BOY . . . OR A GIRL . . . OR WHATEVER IT IS BUT YOU DIDN'T KNOW AND HOLY HELL WE HAVE A BOY . . . OR A GIRL . . . OR WHATEVER

IT IS THE BIGGEST AND BEST SURPRISE EVER IN YOUR WHOLE ENTIRE LIFE!!!!!!!

Now hurry up and get that Facebook post up; people need to know what to buy you!

Instead of onesies we should have just bought
ole Jake back there a haircut.

HE SAID

Finding out the sex of your baby has become an insane, Pinterest-driven spectacle, rivaled only by the NFL Draft. Just the other day on Facebook, I saw that a friend and her husband had invited over more people than Page and I had at our wedding to announce the gender(s?) of their twins. Was it two boys? Two girls? One of each? The thousands on hand waited with baited breath. As I watched one of the seven filmed angles unfold, I realize that they were not going the now-traditional pink/blue cake, cup-cake, or wrapped-box route. No, each spouse knew the sex of one of the twins, and therefore was tasked with buying either a Superman or Superwoman T-shirt, which would be unleashed with the progressive unzipping of their jackets. She went first . . . SUPERMAN! The crowd goes wild. He goes next . . . milking it perfectly . . . then right as the crowd reaches full lather—*BOOM*—another Superman. Twin boys. Over the top? No doubt. But damn, if it wasn't cute as shit.

Page and I did no such thing. Not that we were above it; it was just that we lacked the creativity to come up with a superhero-themed event. Hell, our boys used to ask us for Iron Man and Hulk parties nearly a year in advance for their birthday, and all we were ever able to deliver were mismatched Marvel plates from a non-Avengers movie in the Party City clearance bin. Sorry, kids, I don't give a shit if Iron Man's suit has changed in the forty-seven sequels since.

Page and I mixed it up. We waited to find out the sex of number one and number three, and found out early for number two. I was all-in on Team Find Out, whereas Page was dead set on waiting, so for Ford, our oldest, we waited. It was brutal. I wanted to know so bad. Page would always counter with, "What will knowing the sex now do for you?" To which I would always reply, I'll . . . um . . . know what color to paint . . . things." To which she would always reply, "You can't even paint by numbers." And on and on it would go. I have to admit, the further along we got into the pregnancy, the more I would buy in. A few months later, it's Game Day, and holy hell, I've never been more excited to see a penis in my life. Welcome to Earth, Ford; please excuse the grown man bedside absolutely losing his shit.

For Cal, we found out . . . and if I'm being honest, it sucked. The timing worked so we were able to get a printout from the OB-GYN and wrap it for Christmas. We had family in town for the holidays, so everyone was beside themselves when it came time to open the announcement. IT'S . . . a . . . oh . . . um, it's a boy. Cool.

Finally, for June, you better believe we waited again to find out again, and the process was very similar to Ford's above, except for the whole penis thing. The doc hadn't even finished delivering her before I'd moonwalked into the urologist's office down the hall. *Hallelujah*—it was a girl! Vasectomy time, baby. Time to shut this circus down.

The final verdict? Wait to find out. It's one of life's last true surprises.

PINK OR BLUE? OR GREEN OR YELLOW? — SHE REACTS

Is anyone else starting to see a theme here? Page is right about something. Jake fights it. Years later, Jake admits Page was right and tells some story about how difficult he made life for her anyway at that time. Only fact check in this one: my painting comment comeback surely was better quality than what you wrote. "You can't even paint by numbers"? That's a dad joke. Nice try.

PINK OR BLUE? OR GREEN OR YELLOW? — HE REACTS

To stick with the superhero thread from this chapter—holy hot take, Batman. I feel like we may have struck a chord here. The moral of the story, kids? Don't find out the sex . . . or Page will hunt you down and kill you.

I will say, the car seat/clothes advice Page gives is dead-on. Car seats are only slightly less expensive than ACTUAL CARS. Mother of God. Believe her when she says the clothes will come regardless. For boys, it's a little less exciting—we'll get a tattered jersey or old sneakers every now and then. But for June? Back up the Brink's truck. I'll come home to three to four of those monster black trash bags for yard waste filled with the most elaborate girls' clothing you can imagine.

Surprise sex discovery. Free car seats. Lawn bags filled with clothes. Wash, rinse, repeat. Welcome to the pregnancy circle of life.

CHAPTER 13
This Isn't Registering

SHE SAID

At the start of creating both our wedding registry and our baby registry, Jake grabbed the scanner gun and beelined for the exact same thing: a PlayStation. Or was it an Xbox? Or a Nintendo? Whatever the hell stupid video game thing it was, it was the first thing on his list when we got married *AND* when we reproduced. Sometimes boys are just dumb. For our wedding registry it was funny and odd . . . but actually not the craziest thing in the world. I mean, it's not like I could really argue that a $300 gravy boat would get more use than a gaming console.

Fine.

But when I asked why he thought video game equipment was something that could (let alone *should*) make it onto our baby registry he told me it was so he'd have something to do when he was up in the middle of the night with the baby. I blank-stared him to within an inch of his life. If the baby is up in the middle of the night . . . I patiently explained to him . . . it's because the baby needs something. He's hungry. Or his diaper is wet. Maybe he's got an invisible piece of fuzz stuck in his eye, and he's screaming his head off like an a-hole until the ever-flowing tears push it out and he has exhausted himself back to sleep. But he's probably not up because he wants to help pick your Madden lineup. And as much as I'm sure he'd get a kick out of watching your FIFA world championship banana kick from his bouncy seat, he'd probably prefer an actual snuggle. Perhaps even a rock in the glider while he takes down a bottle of pumped breast milk? But you know what he'll need for any of this night to happen? A glider, a bottle, a breast pump, milk bags, crib sheets, a snuggle blanket, a swaddle blanket, a sleep-sack blanket, diapers, diaper cream, crib sheets, pajamas . . . and the list goes on, and on, and on . . .

My mom's favorite thing to say was always, "All the baby really needs is you." And while that may be all the *baby* needs, that Ergobaby carrier sure as hell does make it easier for YOU to wash dishes while holding a mini human. A thorough baby registry would honestly be longer than this book. You will never think of everything you'll possibly need and want. There will be seven hundred types of pacifiers to choose from, and you will pick the one that gives your kid a mouth sore. There will be sixty-two types of cotton to choose from for crib sheets and you will pick the one that gives your kid a rash. It happens. But it's better than no pacifier or crib sheet at all.

One word of advice for those of you who look to fellow new moms for help on this one: *don't*. Don't ask your friend who just had a baby what she registered for because all of her information will be out of date, like . . . yesterday. When our youngest child was three years old, a friend asked if I could look over her registry to see what she was missing. I didn't even recognize what she had, let alone what she was missing. It was all electronic. It was all personalized. And I'm pretty sure it was all in Swedish. Had I clicked on IKEA by accident? Nope. Babies are just apparently now super into clean lines in their nursery decor and infant gear.

So here's what you can do: Find a friend who is about a month or two ahead of you in her pregnancy. It has to be her first pregnancy, or else she has already lost too many brain cells. Choose the one who got straight A's in school. The one with the alphabetized spice rack. If she's a CPA, a teacher, or works in some type of finance . . . BONUS POINTS. She will have done her homework on safety ratings, and which organic cotton is most hypoallergenic, and conversion vs. traditional cribs, and YES THESE ARE ALL ACTUAL THINGS. And as much as you want to roll your eyes at them you still have to choose. So you take her registry . . . and . . . YOU . . . STEAL . . . IT. All of it. She is smarter and more prepared than you. Pretend you're back in high school, and just look right over her shoulder and copy away. If she's having a boy and you're having a girl, you can change the necessary color schemes around. But if you paid any attention at all to Chapter 12 then you can literally click through and double every glorious gender-neutral choice and basically say "ditto" throughout all of buybuybaby.com.

And just like that, I saved you three weeks' worth of reading online articles about which diaper bag can hold the most boxes of Goldfish. Just imagine how many games of Super Mario you can play in that time . . .

HE SAID

Let me preface this chapter with, *I like to shop.* Literally the day I first drafted this chapter, I asked Page to meet me at the local Lululemon, where I proceeded to take about thirty minutes longer than she did and try on about five things for her and a stylist to comment on. I even asked if they could hem some pants for me. At Lululemon.

Rewind the tape to my marriage "proposal" to Page back in 2006. We had been dating for almost a year, things were clearly serious, the DTR had long since happened, and together we kind of decided to get engaged.

Fortunately, Page was game to register before I put a ring on it. There was a Target and a Bed Bath & Beyond nearby, so we went crazy. The final tally:

Page: One silverware set, bedding, pots, pans, knives . . .

Jake: Twelve Wiis, three TVs, eighteen basketballs . . .

What can I say, I like to shop. Which brings us to registering for our baby shower. On paper, this was a no-brainer; sure, the baby will need some stuff, but people get how hard it is to have a baby. They'll understand why additional video gaming systems are on the list. Why a guy would need a Beer of the Month Club subscription, etc.

Turns out, I'm wrong. People will very much not get that, and by people, I mean women, and by women, I mean mothers. So you mean to tell me I have to register for gifts that I won't ever get to use? Gifts for someone who isn't even born?

PSSSSHT.

Someone has to change this, and if it has to be me, then so be it. I know there are babymoons, diaper parties, and other ways people dress up these pre-baby "your life is about to end" throw-downs, but I'm talking *gifts*. I feel like we should be rewarded for bringing a whining, crying, pooping nuisance into the world. Someone who will trash a stranger's house, puke on call, and stand up half naked in a crowd and yell, "Look at my weewee!"

Wait . . .

Did somebody say, "Wii Wii"?

Exactly.

THIS ISN'T REGISTERING — SHE REACTS

Amen to that. For every gift used just by the baby, there should be a gift used just by the parent. Great call, Jake. Now I want to be showered for having another baby . . . but never to attend another baby shower. Unless I win the lottery between now and then. Oh . . . and it was a Wii! *shrug* Xbox, Wii . . . tomato, tomahto . . .

THIS ISN'T REGISTERING — HE REACTS

I've got your banana kick right here.

The irony of all of this is I haven't played video games in years. Why? Kids. Now Ford and Cal run circles around me. "Pick up your sticks, Dad. Get ready to lose at Madden!" To which I reply, "Yeah, well, if you're not careful, you're gonna have to, um, pick up sticks outside. As yardwork. Which you'll also lose at."

Sigh. I'm not even good at smack talk anymore. This whole dad thing hit me like a ton of bricks . . . sort of like how Mario punches bricks. Dammit, I did it again.

CHAPTER 14
The Babymooners

SHE SAID

Picture it:

White sand beaches.

A warm ocean breeze.

The tinkering sounds of a steel-drum band off in the distance as the sun gently sets . . . and your fat ass huffing and puffing its way out of the sand pit you've been stuck in for the past thirty minutes because your husband went to get himself a beer and must still be chatting it up with the bartender.

The bright side: you're FINALLY not sweating like you just got out of a pool because the God-blessed sun has FINALLY set, but you're still sweating more than . . . well . . . anyone else around you. And dammit, it's been hot all day and you're parched. You want nothing more than an ice-cold refreshing can of . . . LaCroix?

WTF.

Who thought of this babymoon thing, anyway?!

A vacation where you can't sit out in the sun for fear of melasma turning you into a permanent burns-unit victim, you can't wear cute vacation clothes because nothing short of a bed sheet fits you, you're too tired to walk and see any cool sites, and only one of you can drink? NO THANK YOU.

Since having kids, I've often wondered why child-free people need vacations, anyway. You want to go to sleep right now just because you're tired and no one needs a bath, or a book, or help with math you forgot how to do a week after you learned it twenty years ago? Go for it! Your down comforter awaits. Feel like kicking back a few cold ones while you watch football on a Sunday afternoon? Have at it! You don't have to worry that your kid is gonna wake up from his nap/needs a ride somewhere after the game ends/is generally an annoying human being who needs something done RIGHT NOW every time the Panthers make it into the red zone. Want to go out to dinner with friends/alone/ as a couple who actually gets to make eye contact, converse, and (gasp!) listen and laugh with each other WITHOUT having to pay someone to sit and watch TV at your house while your baby sleeps upstairs? By all means, make that reservation, and know that you won't have to cancel because your midget roommate threw up five minutes before it was time to leave, and now you have to give those Beyoncé tickets away to the neighbor kid down the street (#complainingforafriend).

To a child-free person, the world is your vacation. Enjoy it. I mean I hate you, and bite me. But for now . . . enjoy it. You'll join us one of these days and when you do, we'll welcome you with open arms, and a playroom upstairs so we can watch five minutes of the game in relative peace. My point is this: don't waste what's already a vacation-filled life on taking a good one when you least need it. You're still excited about this change. You're pumped to decorate a nursery, shop for miniature clothes, put your feet up to alleviate some of that swelling whenever you need to. Go with that. Save the vacation for after the kid is actually here. A few months in, when you're relatively assured your mother-in-law did, in fact, keep your spouse alive and probably can do the same with your baby. At least, for one long weekend. Save the getaway for when you actually feel the need to do just that. Because after that kid arrives . . . that's when you're really gonna feel the need to escape.

HE SAID

Among the first things I thought upon meeting Page was, "I bet you when we get married, she'll want to do a surprise first wedding dance, post it to YouTube, go viral, get discovered by Rachael Ray, win a dance-off on her show, and take home a trip to Saint Croix that we'll stupidly waste before we have our first kid."

OK, so maybe that's not entirely true . . . but I'll be damned if that's not what happened.

Wind back the clock to 2006; I've got a front spike and Page has a same-sex crush on Missy Elliott. When it came time to discuss our first dance, the decision was clear: "It's either Missy, or I'm bailing on you," Page casually informed me. Misdemeanor it was. One scorched wedding dance floor later, we surprised everyone by transitioning seamlessly from "Unforgettable" to "Lose Control." God, it was amazing.

Right around that time, YouTube was coming into its own, thanks to "Lazy Sunday" and the rest of the SNL gang, and we rode the wave, posting our dance and racking up north of a million views. Eeeeeasy, millennials. That was a lot back then. Rachael Ray's producers took note, and around Valentine's Day 2008, we were invited along with two other couples to compete in a first wedding dance dance-off.

Despite the show not clearing our song and us having to completely make up a new dance to the instrumental beat

Missy sampled in "Lose Control," we crushed it, and took home first place: an all-expenses-paid trip to Saint Croix. Ho. Lee. Shitballs.

If only all of the above had gone down in 2007.

The rules stated that we had to take the trip in 2008, so by that fall, Page was about five months pregnant with Ford. You know, perrrrrfect timing for essentially a second honeymoon. Not to worry, we were told, this would be a perrrrrfect excuse for a babymoon. A . . . babymoon?

Apparently, this is a thing. A dumb thing. I mean, don't get me wrong; it was an amazing trip. The weather was freaking perfect, and on the heels of a hurricane that had just blown through, the resort was deserted. We had the place to ourselves. That said, all I could think about was how miserable Page must have been.

"Page, care to join me in drinking these all-inclusive beers? No? OK, I've got it."

"Page, care to join me outside in this one-hundred-degree weather? No? OK, I'll be back in a few."

"Page, care for a Corona—what's that? I've already offered you drinks? OK, never mind."

"Page, care to take the next flight home?"

Look, we had an awesome time (even despite the hefty tax bill that came our way four months later), but my advice—if you're planning one of these babymoons—would be to pump the brakes a bit. Maybe don't go to a beautiful island resort for a week. Maybe instead opt for one of the *New York Times'* "36 Hours" trips . . .

. . . to Cleveland.

*Still smiling after our big win . . . because it would be a year
before we realized how much our "prize" was gonna cost us.*

THE BABYMOONERS — SHE REACTS

Three kids in, and I'd gladly take a trip to Cleveland . . . as long as they *aren't invited. And thank you for being aware of how much that vacation kind of sucked for me. But as much as I like to complain about it for the sake of this chapter, what I remember most from that babymoon is that I felt Ford kick for the first time while we were there. It was my FAVORITE. Sweetest thing ever. And there was only a miniscule chance it was the island food or contaminated water that made my stomach jump and twist like that, as opposed to those first baby kicks.*

THE BABYMOONERS — HE REACTS

Beyoncé, huh? Well, that escalated quickly.

You're so right about DINKs. Tuesdays are a vacation. You and I hate Tuesdays.

It reminds me of the time—and this would be perfect for the next book we write about raising toddlers, set for a 2037 release— we went to Jamaica with our family for Christmas. Ford and Cal were BABIES, and we were the only ones there with kids. Look, it was Jamaica, so it was great, but otherwise, it was decidedly not great. There was a pool, rocky cliffs, sharp edges, etc., and on top of that, family members who had absolutely zero interest in babysitting (who could blame them). On the last day of the trip, we were talking to my uncle about how great the house, chefs, and service were, and I'll never forget his response: "Yeah, and they tried to offer us nannies too, but I told them, no, thanks; we're not THOSE people."

There . . . were . . . NANNIES?!

Spoiler alert: we're those people.

THIRD TRIMESTER

Are We There Yet?

CHAPTER 15
The Best-Laid Plans

SHE SAID

OK. Let me just tell you this up front. I am very organized. Like . . . VERY organized. My pantry is labeled. My closet is color-coded. My shirts hang long sleeve, to short sleeve, to sleeveless, etc. I'm no stranger to structure. Or logic. Or commonsense. Which is why even as an organized, logical, commonsensical (is that even a word?) person, I saw zero point in putting together a birth plan. Babies and their comings and goings (in this case goings) are none of those things. So why put together a "plan" just so they can shit all over it? Believe me, they will be shitting all over enough things when they get here. Don't allow them the satisfaction of doing it to this, too.

Your doctors, of course, will tell you otherwise. "Have a plan," they'll say. "Write it down," they'll say. "That way, when you go into labor, you won't have to make decisions on the fly, and the medical staff will know what you want."

Horse.

Shit.

All of it.

The medical staff just wants to keep you and your baby alive and preferably happy enough that you won't sue them afterward. And the baby, for sure, won't care what you want.

If your "plan" is to have a home water birth with no drugs and live "Kumbaya" music playing in the background, I guarantee there will be a drought the month you're due. Your county will be put on a water restriction so you can't fill up anything. Even at-home baby pools in your living room. And yes, "they" will know if you do!

You won't go into labor on your own so will have to be induced (drug #1).

It will be so hard, and fast, and painful (and yet unproductive in terms of moving labor along) that you'll scream out for seventeen epidurals (drugs #2–17).

Still, nothing will happen.

Speaking of nothing happening, you wish that was the case for the hospital sound system. A button will have gotten pushed down and stuck on the heavy metal station. You're trying to hear an "ooommmmmm" through it all, but in your actual ears Axl Rose is screaming, "Welcome to the Jungle" over your head while you almost split in two.

Doc says the baby's heartbeat is dropping (in spite of the excitement of the live Guns-n-Roses concert he's been listening to).

Time for a C-section.

You're starting to feel things again below the waist, so they have to knock you out quick (what drug # are we up to now, 100?). Baby comes out cute as a button (no birth canal conehead for this little one), and high as a kite. (I'm kidding, you druggie. Re-LAAAX.) You get one of those awkward baby-at-your-shoulder newborn pics where any way you look at it either you or the baby is upside down. Fast forward a couple hours and you are in a world of pain. You know what that means. PERCOSET. OK, maybe now you really do have a problem . . .

I think our OB office actually gave us a pamphlet to fill out for our birth "plan." Ha! It had questions to consider like:

"What type of lighting would you prefer?"

"Do you want music on or off?"

"Where should your partner stand?"

I'm sorry. Are we planning for childbirth or our wedding processional?

I think the only question I actually answered was, "Are you planning for a natural childbirth (no drugs), or would you like an epidural?" I simply wrote the word *"EPIDURAL"* across every page, regardless of the actual subject matter. I wrote it in fourteen languages. I used a black Sharpie. And guess what? In two out of three of my births, the epidural wore off, and I felt EVERY M-EFFING THING.

People, let's be real. The only part of this you can "plan" is whether or not you get pregnant in the first place. Hence the title of this chapter. And even *that* is a huge question mark. Yes . . . to *some* extent you can at least *try* to plan when you **don't** want to get pregnant. But after it happens, the rest is kind of up to chance. When in doubt, go with the old adage, "Plan for the worst, hope for the best." That way you can only be pleasantly surprised instead of shockingly disappointed and depressed. But if you feel more of the latter, don't worry, there are drugs for that too.

HE SAID

Oh, hi, Third Trimester, I didn't see you there. What's that? Now's the time when we should actually start planning things? When we should start packing a bag and writing a birth plan? There are also mandatory birthing classes we have to attend with weird, fake, non-blinking babies and videos starring actors with unkempt pubes?

At this point, with all rational thoughts completely out the window, this advice seems completely normal. You're brainwashed into thinking all of this is necessary, and in fact, if you don't do it, the delivery will be an epic failure. Well I'm here to help demystify the process. Let's walk through the three Ps of planning. And no, *pubes* is not one.

PLAN

Yes, I realize the first P of *planning* is *plan* . . . this sounded better in my head . . . but that's short for *birth plan*. You know, that thirty-seven-hundred-page document the hospital not-so-gently suggests you draft, have notarized, custom-frame, and memorize as if it's your last rights? We were reminded of this document so much, in fact, that I started having nightmares about it:

Doc: "Ma'am, please hand me your birth plan."

Page: "We don't have one."

audible gasps

Doc: *slowly removes glasses* "Well . . . then . . . I'm not sure how I'm going to do this."

Page: "Do . . . what? Deliver the baby? Aren't you a—"

Doc: "Shut your mouth, you animal. You should be ashamed of yourselves . . . *no plan?!* Jesus . . ."

slaps off surgical gloves, exits

Jake (to Page): "I told you s—"

Then I wake up . . . always with a dull pain in my ribs. Hmmm.

Would you like a natural birth? Put it in the plan. Oh, interesting, you crave pain? Put it in the plan. You also hate Pitocin? Put it in the plan. OK, wow, you don't you want an epidural either? Plan. Has anyone called the anesthesiologist yet, you know, just in case? Piggity piggity plan. You really seem like you're in an enormous amount of agony, this is just for show at this point, right? Put that sucka in tha plan.

I vaguely remember Page and I talking about, or even starting to draft a plan, but, of course, we couldn't take ourselves seriously.

2:00 p.m.: Water breaks at home, flooding the hardwoods.

2:01 p.m.: Drive 145 mph to hospital.

2:04 p.m.: Dramatically wheel Page into delivery room, screech wheelchair to a halt, momentum delivers baby directly into doc's arms.

2:09 p.m.: Done. No pain, no mess, healthy baby.

2:15 p.m.: Home, baby sleeps through the night immediately.

The end.

Needless to say, our expectations were off by a hair. But apparently, some of these things can get extremely detailed. I can't imagine a doctor in that scenario . . . the baby is coming out . . . there are complications . . . I mean, seriously, do the parents, in the moment, say, "Stick to the plan . . . stick to the plan!"—like Mel Gibson in the famous *Braveheart* battle scene: "Hold! Holllld! HOLLLLLLLD!!" At some point, doesn't the doctor just yell, "EFF YOUR PLAN, WOMAN!!" and do his/her thing?

At the end of the day, have a loose outline for things in case you want someone to, oh, I don't know, bring you mint chocolate chip ice cream within seven minutes of delivery (ahem, Page), but if you're a crazy, birth plan stick-to-er, just know that karma has set the over/under line for your hours of labor at 39.5.

PREP

The final few months of pregnancy are all about the prep. You prep the house, the nursery, the car, the vagina. You clean, you reorganize, you bubble wrap everything. All done? Rinse and repeat for all four locations.

Never in my life have I ever prepped for anything more. Ever. In my life. You know in the Olympics when the 100-meter dash sprinters take their marks? There's always that one Ukrainian sprinter with zero self-awareness, who everyone knows is finishing last, that takes FOREVER to get ready in the blocks. The guy that makes everyone else wait while he gets absolutely perfectly ready. That wait feels like an eternity to me every time I watch it. It's what, like, three seconds?

Now imagine holding your mark in the blocks for, like, *nine months.*

That's what the prep process felt like to me.

"Have you talked to the hospital to make sure we're all set?"

"Yes, a couple months ago, honey."

"OK, well, do we have the correct car seats?"

"Yes, love; don't you remember us spending the GDP of Sweden on them last weekend? And don't you remember taking them to the highest-rated fire department on Yelp to have them installed? Anything else, sweetie?"

"Ah, OK, good . . . um . . . have you gone back through the birth plan just to be sure we didn't miss anything?"

"Yep, doing that now, let me just print it out and . . . jump out of this window. Byyyeeeee."

For us, the prep process differed between kids, too. If you remember from a few chapters ago—or not, if you've got preggo/newborn brain—for Ford and June, we waited to find out the sex. It was magical. For Cal, we put a pic from the OB-GYN under the Christmas tree. I thought I was Team Find Out . . . until we opened that envelope to find Cal's blurry, dancing, black-and-white sugarplums. We hugged, shook hands, and quickly moved on to dinner. I think I've celebrated more following staff meetings.

Friendly reminder: if there's one thing you take away from this book, please let it be to wait to find out your baby's sex. It's worth every agonizing day you wait. And I was wrong in thinking it would be anything otherwise.

So there, Page, I can admit I was wrong . . .

. . .

. . .

. . . as long as you admit that spending time prepping for the babies was wrong, too . . .

ducks

PACK

This section is on the bag. The f#%(^%#^*ing bag.

"Pack a bag," they say.

"You'll want it in the hospital," they say.

"It'll be a lifesaver," they say.

You'll actually never even glance at the bag once at any point during the course of your hospital stay unless it's full of phone chargers and donuts . . . they never say.

In case you're thoroughly confused, "the bag" is what every book, video, and Pinterest-obsessed friend of your wife's encourages you to pack for the hospital. Whether you have an emergency C-section or a super-smooth fifteen-minute delivery (Ha.), the bag will help you navigate all that the baby-delivery process throws your way.

Until your wife shits on the delivery table while pushing.

Whatchya got now, bag?!

You should have seen the bag Page and I packed for Ford's delivery. Thirty-plus DVDs, a speaker dock for my iPhone, a camcorder (Jesus, I sound old here), towels, sheets, a Honey Baked Ham, our old high school yearbooks, our cat, and like fourteen bags of candy. Unless instant diabetes was on the docket, I have no idea what we had hoped to accomplish with this bag.

Regardless, it was packed, and we were ready.

Fast-forward to the big day, and unfortunately, while it wasn't diabetes, it was close—Page was hit with rapid-onset preeclampsia, and our doc said, "DO NOT PASS GO. DO NOT COLLECT $200. GO STRAIGHT TO THE HOSPITAL."

Because we had been beaten into submission over the bag by this point, I cannot be blamed for what I uttered next:

"Do we have time to go home and get our bag?"

The doc was not amused.

We didn't see that freaking bag until three days later. Baby in hand. The moral of the story, kids? Refrigerate the ham . . . sorry, no, the moral is, you don't need the bag.

So there you have it. The three P's of baby planning demystified: Plan, prep, and pack.

(Then throw it all out the window.)

THE BEST-LAID PLANS — SHE REACTS

And heeerrrrre's where we start to fall into lots of agreement. Babies and their shitting on of plans. And the uselessness of the plans. But I did no packing of a bag. Must have been all you? And it was a TUNA SUB FROM JERSEY MIKE'S (Mike's way—light on the liquids, add pickles and yellow mustard) that I demanded post-delivery. Not mint-chocolate-chip ice cream. Hmmm . . . maybe we should learn to write some things down, after all.

THE BEST-LAID PLANS — HE REACTS

Reading that you agree with me so wholeheartedly on the plan, I have to wonder, who actually uses one of these things? Are there really scenarios out there where a couple 100 percent dictates a delivery based on this thing? Or, even weirder, are there third parties who do this?!

I'm picturing a friend of the soon-to-be mom's standing bedside with a long scroll. "Ah, no, sorry, John . . . the foot massage comes at hour eight. If you could throw on some Erykah Badu and fire up some lobster mac 'n' cheese for us, that would be great. It's what Karen and the baby want, after all."

CHAPTER 16
Deliverance

SHE SAID

Buckle up, folks. Shit's about to get REAL.

Delivery is where it all goes down. And out. And I do mean *all of it*. At least, some of the time. More on that in a bit . . .

First up, if you've read the last chapter on your delivery "plans," you already know you can go ahead and wipe your ass with those. Assuming you make it to a healthy full-term pregnancy, you have about a five-week window in which you can safely assume at some point this baby will exit your body somehow. Outside of that, you know squat.

When I was about thirty-eight weeks pregnant with Ford, I was at home in the middle of putting away a load of laundry when I realized I was late for an OB checkup. Stacks of sorted clothes were all over the counters. Chicken was defrosting in the sink. I hadn't washed my hair in three days. Whatevs. *I'll get to all that when I get back,* I thought, as I threw on a XXXL sweatshirt and heaved myself into the car. Fast-forward to twenty minutes later, my blood pressure clocks in as high upon arrival and the doc tells us to, "Head on over to deliver now." All casual-like, as if she'd suggested an easy recipe to try for dinner that night.

"I'm sorry, *what?*"

She repeated herself again. Something along the lines of, "blood pressure high . . . baby . . . deliver now." We asked if we could swing by the house to grab the bag we'd packed. (We were LYING. I was not a bag pre-packer. And in my ignorance of Jake's impressive pre-prep work, I found myself wondering if FOR THE LOVE—can a sister at least go snag a nightgown and some cozy socks for the hospital stay?) No. We could not. It was straight to the hospital and do not pass go.

OKAAAAAAAY.

I immediately called my mom and told her to start driving down from DC and to FREAK OUT BECAUSE WTF DO I KNOW ABOUT GIVING BIRTH AND HOW AM I GONNA KNOW WHAT TO DO?!?!?! She forgave the f-bomb. After all, she knew what was coming. And if ever an f-bomb is warranted . . .

The thirty seconds it took us to cross the street from my OB's office to the hospital led to thirteen (Fourteen? Fifteen? . . .) hours of waiting. And waiting. And very uncomfortably waiting. I was induced all three times and all three times it took almost fifteen hours for the Pitocin to do its thing. It took the epidural, however, only about five minutes to wear off. I'm the same with anesthesia at the dentist. I always start to feel stuff about halfway through. It's *super* pleasant. But I should have known. Apparently I metabolize everything quickly except food. Sweet.

They say you forget the pain of childbirth and that that's why women go on to have more than one child. "They" are incorrect. I still vividly remember twisting Jake's T-shirt into my fists and screaming out, "ring of FIIIIIIIIIIRE," on repeat when Ford was crowning. I will never forget envisioning my entire body being split in two during June's birth and having the most genuine desire to shove the entire baby back into my body and remain pregnant for all of eternity rather than push the shoulders out of whatever massive monster-being's head had just warriored its way out of my vagina.

I will spare you the (rest of the) details of each birth because I still want you to go through with this. The second time around, I'd learned to ask for an epidural redo to the point that I was so numb, I couldn't move my own legs. Perfect. Third time around was the only one where I pushed out more than just the baby during delivery. So, yes, you can make it a few go-rounds without pooping during your delivery, but don't get too cocky. Poopless deliveries were my claim to fame, and look where that got me.

Some of you will have super-easy births. Some of you will experience the stuff of horror films. Some will deliver in the waiting room, or on the highway, or during a preplanned trip to an operating room with a team of doctors and masks and your spleen sitting on your right shoulder for a quick sec while the doc pulls your baby into the world.

*Sidenote on that: the favorite part of any dad-birth rendition that involves a C-section is seeing all of his wife's innards pulled-and-plopped outside her body while the doc delivers. The not-even-remotely-close-to-being-favorite part of any dad-birth rendition that involves a vaginal birth is what appears to be seeing all of his wife's innards expand, and explode, and just generally contort in ways that could rival Cirque du Soleil. A word to the wise: when you're folded into a human pretzel, there is no such thing as staying "up by her head." When her head is folded all the way directly into her crotch, you are going to see her vagina explode. You just are. So let me take this moment to remind us all that it was that vagina and your desire to be so close to it that got us all into this mess in the first place. And in spite of your concerns that if you see it in this state, you won't want to get that close to it again, YOU WILL. And, frankly, it will probably be far sooner than the woman attached to that vagina is ready for after said explosion. So hold your ground (and that leg, while you're there) and just get over it. Because the only way to be that close to the baby when it comes out is to be that close to where the baby comes out.

Take a cue from the circus. Step right up! Come see the show! The prize at the end is worth seeing the House of Horrors on the way there.

HE SAID

The movies are a load of crap.

I was under the impression there was a dramatic, mid-sentence water breakage, a mad dash to the hospital, a near delivery during a speeding wheelchair scene, and then a nice and nifty forty-five–second labor, with maybe a few PG-13 swear words. Four hours later, you're home, and life is off and running, smooth as can be.

Inaccurate.

While things weren't exactly peachy for us, they also weren't insanely dramatic. At all. For the most part. I'm pretty sure. Wait. Now that I think back, I probably should have been more concerned. I should probably shut up now.

I think the best way to describe the holy-shit-fasten-your-safety-belt part of this journey is by walking you through what I experienced and learned from each of our deliveries, broken into the only four categories that matter to this story: the arrival, the wait, and the delivery.

FORD

Arrival: Well, you already know how we ended up at the hospital. The day started innocently enough, until Page's blood pressure hit 109.7, forty-five gallons of fluid collected in her ankles, and her face turned a color I can only categorize as sandy plum. One swift kick to the rear and a "JUST FORGET THE EFFING BAG ALREADY" from our OB later, we were at the hospital.

Wait: Pitocin, meet the Fehlings. Fehlings, Pitocin. GOOD LORD, did we wait long. Thanks for nothing, drugs. They made this stuff sound like it was the baby-delivery equivalent to prune juice. Except in this case, there was no diarrhea, er, baby for HOURS. We watched movies, we—*gasp!*—talked, we reminisced on our old life. "Remember when we used to go to movies?" *Sigh.* "Yeah. Remember when we . . . wait . . . was that a contraction . . .?"

Delivery: Apparently epidurals have an expiration date. Or, take a while to kick in. Either way, Page was starting to feel things. And getting really nervous about what that could mean if the labor drew on. Fortunately, it didn't, and about thirty minutes later, out popped Ford. Even writing that just now gave me goose bumps. There's nothing like experiencing that first delivery. Add in the fact that we were waiting to find out the sex . . . and, *man,* what a special, special moment. OK, let's bring the jokes back; it's getting misty in here . . .

CAL

Arrival: Whereas Ford came a week early amid a wave of high blood pressure, Cal was straight CHILLIN' in the womb. He did get our attention about a month before D-Day, again due to a BP spike, but that all calmed down during the homestretch. The docs eventually scheduled a delivery day for us, and—bag in tow!—we strolled into the hospital. We were pros at this point, nodding at security guards and nurses, all of whom returned a "I don't know you, but we look forward to seeing your vagina later" nod of recognition.

Wait: Yet again, we spiral into a Pitocin-induced boredom. Oh, I'm sorry, you thought it induced labor? LOLZ. Hour after hour rolls by, and in her delirium, Page somehow orders two epidurals. Not joking. She was not going to mess around with a newborn who was a week overdue and had a Fehling head. Meanwhile, our doc decided that peppering me with questions about my job at USA Baseball was a good look while Page slowly crept into labor. It was not. I'm pretty sure he was one fun fact about the Yankees closer situation away from Page activating Pregnant Serial Killer mode.

Delivery: If "Gurrrl, that's a helluva epidural" doesn't adorn Page's tombstone someday, then I don't know what will. Long story short, Page delivered Cal after another thirty-minute round of labor. Cal was ten pounds, six ounces, and Page felt nothing. NOTHING. Cal was a grown-ass man at birth. He strolled out of Page with a cognac and mustache, and one of our nurses uttered the famous phrase above in disbelief. At the other end of the bed, Page had no idea what was happening. "What are those noises? Am I still pushing? Where are my legs?" The best I could muster was, "You did great, babe. You basically just delivered Don Draper."

JUNE

Arrival: Once again, a scheduled delivery. Yawn. I guess a high-stakes, 100-mph police chase to the hospital wasn't in the cards for us. I'm sure Page spends much of her downtime lamenting the fact that her water didn't break in a crowded restaurant.

Wait: The Pitocin actually worked this time, so our wait wasn't incredibly long. I'm sure there were other highlights along the way, and the drama around "willitbeagirl–willitbeagirl–willitbe-agirl–willitbeagirl" was palpable, but all I can really remember from the wait was watching *Tommy Boy*. I know—random. But get this: a few minutes in, Page says, "I'm . . . I'm not sure if I've ever seen this." Then, a few more minutes later, she says, "So . . . 'Holy Shnikees!' isn't original? You didn't make that up?" Uh-oh. My life flashed before my eyes . . . and then she said it: "So, your whole shtick is ripped from this movie? Are you not really funny, after all?"

There was only one way to counter: "Are you talking?"

Delivery: Did I say the movies are B.S.? Well, maybe I should take that back. Ladies and Gentlemen, this delivery checked EVERY. SINGLE. BOX. Shorter wait time? Check. Longer labor? Check? Expired epidural? Check. Screaming bloody murder? Check. Poop? CHECK! Finally, on baby number three, Page got her Oscar. And we got our girl.

DELIVERANCE — SHE REACTS

My old boss once recommended to me that we write down the stories of our kids' births. She said it was always her kids' favorite thing to hear on their birthdays. Of course, Jake and I never really did. So maybe we'll read them these. "Dearest children, you entered the world amid comparisons of houses of horror, comedy knuckleheads, and public defecation. HAPPY BIRTHDAY TO YOU!"

DELIVERANCE — HE REACTS

Super-casual "sidenote" you dropped on the dads there at the end. Maybe instead lead with "Warning:" or "You may want to stop eating immediately." Please do me a favor, and let me handle all communication with men going forward, thank you very much.

Also, Ring of Fire, Monster Beings, *and* Vagina Warriors *are the trilogy you now HAVE to write: "A series of books for aspiring mothers who REALLY want to be talked out of the whole thing."*

Cal Draper, 5 minutes old. Someone get this man an Old Fashioned.

CHAPTER 17

BOOM.

SHE SAID

Wailing. Screams. Alternating gasps, sighs, and other sounds you don't even know how to categorize. Goo and tears and pee and poop everywhere. This is what's happening in the delivery room after delivery. And just wait till you hear what the baby is like!

People, it is MADNESS. In the most fabulous of ways. But also in the most bizarre. When Ford came out, they put him on my chest, and he gazed up at me with the kindest, most loving look in his eyes. Blinked a few times, then let out something just above a whimper to let us know that yes, he was breathing, and yes, he was also content. He wanted to snuggle. And to this day, he's the tenderest of my three in terms of physical affection. Cal came out the size of a middle-aged man with a side part and potbelly to match. All 10.5 pounds of him roared into the world with an extra-bright spotlight that hasn't stopped shining since. I don't remember June's first five minutes on Earth because I'm pretty sure I blacked out when I registered there was no penis on this one. Praise be. Off Jake went to the vasectomy store.

But back to the baby and what it's like when he/she is finally here . . .

First you push, or they pull, what appears to be an alien frog covered in curdled milk out of your body. Within seconds (after vacuuming out its nose and mouth, and scrubbing it down until it goes from outer-space animal to earthling guinea pig), they tell you to stick your boob in its mouth and "just let nature take its course." WHAT? This is honestly the weirdest part. And while I may not exactly be one to helm the La Leche League meeting, I will say I came to very much love the sweet bonding time of breastfeeding. But the first time you try to shove your nipple into a baby's face, it just feels strange, plain and simple—not to mention the audience of nurses and sometimes close relatives with a front-row seat to the show. Lemme tell you, you better hope the baby gets it right, too. Because otherwise, the lactation consultant steps in. Thankfully, my kids were chowhounds from the start. Somehow though, when I had Cal, I got put on the LC list, and she came by for a "checkup" to make her presence known.

Door opens.

Shadow cast.

It. Is. Large.

Nurse Ratched—er . . . the lactation consultant—enters and goes straight for my boob. More precisely, she went straight for the part they suck on. The areola is the darker circle around the sticky-outie part, right? So what's the sticky-outie part called? Whatever it's called, that's the part she went for, hard and fast. She was like a nipple ninja. She grabbed a hold. "Hi. It's nice to meet you . . .," by the way. "My name is . . ." Nope. There was none of that. Just sticky-outie nerp grab and puuuuuuuulllll until that thing was halfway to Arizona.

"You need to make the nipple easy to get to," she explained. "So when the baby takes it in his mouth he'll get it full all the way to the back of the throat."

Never mind that with the way she was pulling, my baby was gonna get it all the way to the back of his navel. Also never mind the fact that I DID NOT ASK FOR, NEED, OR WANT her "help." Need I remind you I had given birth to someone who looked like he'd just left the buffet and was late to a three o'clock board meeting?

But I suppose it's better to have too much help, rather than not enough. Take, for example, the nighttime nursery. Now THERE is some useful extra help. I had been given opposite of advice on this one. Shocking, I know.

Some said DO IT. "It will save your sanity at least those first few days, and you'll need that extra sleep for when you're home and totally on your own."

Some said DON'T DO IT: "You need to bond with your baby—" but then I tuned out the rest because the first group already had me at "extra sleep."

Now, I've heard some nasty, horrible rumors that some of the hospitals around us don't offer this option anymore. Their reason being that they want the mothers to bond with their babies. Well. Isn't that convenient how our bonding needs to coincide so precisely with their budget cuts. Let me tell you I sent all three of my babies to every minute of the night nursery that they were allowed, and given enough time to sniff me out and do a height check, they'd positively ID me in a mommy line up at least 53 percent of the time. Not bonded, my ass. Or my nipple, depending on who's asking.

HE SAID

Forget *Holy Crap, You're Pregnant.* We've officially crossed over into *Holy Crap, You're a Parent* territory. Nothing prepares you for the moment your baby is born. Nothing. It would be like someone handing you a Rubik's Cube to solve while you try to find one item at Ikea, knowing only the name of the product. "Oh, we need a Kallax for the living room? Sure, no problem. I'll be back in sixty-four years."

All three of our baby welcome parties were incredible in their own right, and I'll admit, I got all sappy about our firstborn in the last chapter, but when it comes to *final push, baby's out, first cry, OMG, BOOM you're a parent* moments, it would be hard to top our grand finale—Miss June.

"Call it, Dad."

I'll never forget that sentence from our delivery nurse.

It was May 17, 2013, and we're welcoming June Elizabeth Fehling into the world . . . except that I can't tell that it's June, let alone a girl, yet . . .

I'm looking for the rare Fehling Double Vagina. And with only seconds remaining, there's no sign of it.

Finally, with the clock ticking and the baby almost out, I see it. No penis. All vag. The ~~curse~~ streak was broken.

What a surreal moment.

Grandparents flooded the room, and my mom promptly passed out when she learned that not only was it a girl, but that we named her after her mom, and that June's middle name was my mom's first name. Night-night, Liz. Tears flowed, hugs were exchanged. And then we handed her off and slept.

Wait, what?

To understand what I mean, you have to turn back the clock even further, to Ford's—our first's—delivery.

For your firstborn, you don't know what you don't know. And my goodness, what rookies we were. That first night, they asked us if we wanted to sleep; they would watch Ford, they explained, and only wake Mom to feed him. We thought they were psychos and declined the offer. Give up our newborn to complete strangers?! You animals!

W. T. F. were we thinking.

Looking back, this makes me laugh. I know what you're going to say: "I was under the impression there would be no advice in this book." Well, OK, that's mostly true . . . but here's a little: DO take them up on that offer to watch your baby at night. They're better at it than you on that first go-round, they change diapers, they do everything, and, most importantly, again, THEY LET YOU SLEEP.

That's the major headline, but here's some bonus advice! DON'T take them up on the offer for baby pictures. Just trust me. Babies are cute, but their fingernails are tiny guillotines, and they don't discriminate where they chop. Which includes the face.

Ford was no different. He chainsaw massacred his little baby grill beyond recognition, and only ceased slicing juuuuuust before the photographer showed up. After the pics developed, and while we waited for child protective services to arrive, Page and I liquidated what money we had left after the deductible for copies of those pics. My God, were we suckers.

With Cal, we learned our lesson. No baby at night. No pictures. No more finding out the sex of the baby. We also learned to just relax. He's not latching? OK, big deal—he'll figure it out. Who's watching Ford? Who cares—the grands have him. We think.

While I do tell people that going from zero to one kid was tough, two to three was tougher, and that one to two was toughest (freaking man-to-man D!), it was in the moment that we had Cal in the hospital that it sunk in that we really were doing this parenting thing . . . and that we were going to be OK.

It was also when we made firm plans to wait more than forty-five seconds between having children on the next round.

BOOM. — SHE REACTS

I love you dearly, my sweet husband. And thank you for either the intentional protective fib or the post-birth brain fart that led you to believe we kept Ford with us overnight in the hospital after he was born . . . but we most certainly did NOT. I will credit us with at least letting it occur to us, "Should we send him to the nursery in between feedings or keep him with us?" the first time around. But we came to a quick (See ya, Ford!) decision then and for the subsequent three. I really don't think there was anything wrong with it . . . or that he looks THAT much like that lady who was in the room next to mine. I mean, they do have those little baby bassinet name tags that stay on pretty well, right?

BOOM. — HE REACTS

"The La Leche League?" Even though you're fluent in Spanish, I can't blame you for the double "the's" there. My mind would totally be a mess too if I had to, um, have my nipples yanked to Arizona and what not.

Good to see we agree on the night nurse, although not so good to see we disagree on how we handled Ford. I remember like it was yesterday: the idea of giving up our baby freaked us out. I definitely went into Irrational New Dad mode and broke out my dad voice.

"Hey, guys, would you like us to watch Ford tonight so you can sleep?"

"(AHEM) NO, THANK YOU; WE'RE JUST FINE. OUR SON WOULD LIKE TO STAY WITH HIS MOTHER." Or something like that.

Breaks the no-looking rule and glances at your response Wait, are we having a fight in our own book? You went all caps on me!!! This is probably unprofessional.

CHAPTER 18
Lucy, I'm Home!

SHE SAID

You did it. Congratulations. You brought a life ... or two lives ... or three lives ... God help you if that list doesn't cover your situation yet ... into this world. You managed to survive *yourselves AND* keep a baby alive while in a hospital with round-the-clock help and a seventeen-to-one ratio of adults to babies. Now you get to go home with this oooing, cooing, snuggling, pooping, crying, soft, warm lump of a human who can't actually verbalize its needs for another two years.

Good luck with that.

We brought all three of our babies home to the same house in Raleigh. It was a sweet little white house with black shutters and a red door. It was on a quiet little cul-de-sac. A *very* quiet little cul-de-sac. A mind-numbingly quiet, boring, nothing ever happened on it to break up my days stuck at home with a newborn, cul-de-sac.

We lived there for about seven years. I'm pretty sure I spent five of those seven years on the same red chair in the living room with either a baby or a pump on my boob. But the other two were spent playing trucks on the floor across the living room, wiping up blackbean smooodge from the countertops . . . the walls . . . and those little crevices that highchairs specialize in, and eventually (finally!) doing full costume changes on June with every single diaper change because there are just so many pink ruffles and hair-flair options out there.

Just know this . . .

There will be sleepless nights. There will be diaper blowouts every time you're going somewhere that punctuality matters. There will be vomiting; and tears; and diarrhea; and pink eye; and hand, foot, and mouth disease (It's a thing. Look it up.); and you will never again buy nice home decor in good conscience. There will be nights when you shove your infant into your spouse's arms and hide in your closet for fifteen minutes with a bottle of Yellow Tail Chardonnay and a bag of carrots and hummus (I've heard). But you are being given the most stupendously mind-bogglingly beautiful privilege in the world, and you will love this little person more than you'd ever thought possible.

You're pregnant.

You're going to have a baby.

Congratulations!!

And HOLY CRAP.

The sweet little white house...

*... and the red chair in the living room where
I (and Ford?) spent so much time.*

HE SAID

I remember when the hospital eventually cut us loose. It was such a bizarre feeling. I never wanted to leave that room. Forget that it was larger than most hotel rooms and the food was sneeeaaaaky good, but it was also safe. We had backups. People watching out for us. Go home? As in, to our actual home with no nurses? AND NO FREE JELLO? Pass.

But it was true. After about seventy-two hours, in came the wheelchair and out go the Fehlings. We were on our way. Before we get into what it was like to cross over the threshold and into the house for the first time, though, can we talk about the wheelchair ride?

I feel like this has the potential to become a *Seinfeld* bit, so I'll dial it back, but . . . Page could have easily walked out all three times, unless I'm completely missing something. I'm sure there is some health-related rule here, but between the wheelchair and the silent, knowing nods we exchanged with the nurses on the way out, it felt like Page was getting honorably discharged from the battlefield. We delivered a baby; we didn't return home from a war.

As soon as we cleared the waiting room, up Page popped, thus commencing Operation Initial Car Seat Install. Just when you think having a fire department help you install your car seat is the most emasculating thing you'll ever do, try getting a seven-pound squirming bag of sugar into a car seat. With the entire hospital waiting room watching. And your parents. And your wife. Who is now really playing the whole thing up by sitting back down in the wheelchair.

With Ford finally secured, I aggressively mouthed toward the waiting room windows: "SOMEDAY YOU'LL BE READING MY BOOK ABOUT THIS... YEAH!... YOU'LL SEE!!" Unfortunately nothing is more awkward looking than aggressively mouthing a long sentence, so they only stared more. I wished them all a bumpy wheelchair ride three days from then and bid everyone adieu.

Out we pulled into traffic, where we promptly caused gridlock. Seventeen MPH in a 55 while straddling two lanes at 5:05 p.m. on a Wednesday is cool, right? Sure, having a kid is a big deal, but is it such a big deal that you should forget how to function as a human? Apparently, *yes,* as it took us roughly eight hours to make our 1.7-mile drive home.

I teased it earlier, but maaaaaaan, those first steps into the house, baby in tow, nurses not in tow, were real. Like, *for real* real. I should have been prepared—my boss at the time warned me about that very thing. "Wait until you get home," he said. "The diapers aren't free anymore."

Forget the diapers, what about—wait, "Page . . . is he breathing? Seriously, get over here . . . wait, no, grab a spoon . . . A SOUP SPOON, NOT A BREAKFAST SPOON, DAMMIT, ARE YOU FREAKING SERIOUS?! . . . Hold it up. Hold it up, yes . . . OK . . . Thank God, it fogged. He's breathing." OK, sorry, where were we?

Ah, yes, the empty home. The uncertainty. The *holy shit*ness.

Can I tell you something, though? You get over it pretty quickly. It's like asking that one friend that everyone has who seems to know how to do everything. Amazing cook. Remodels bathrooms. Fixes engines. And every time you ask him how he learned those things, he says, "Ah, man, I just started doing it, you know?" No, Chris, I don't know. I don't know at all.

Well, much like with your annoying friend, there are no instructions that come with raising a kid, let alone surviving those first few days. We put diapers on upside down and inside out. We gave Ford rashes that I'm pretty sure he's still dealing with today. It was a mess, but we survived. And you will too.

The other thing that helped us hit our stride was some advice we got early on: your baby will sleep about twenty-nine hours a day in those first couple months, so you can still go on dates. GO ON DATES?! But it was true—we went to movies, restaurants and breweries, and Ford slept through it all. It was incredible. It was looking like this parenting thing might not be so bad after all.

And then he turned three months, and . . . well . . .

And then we had two more, and . . . well . . .

HOLY. CRAP.

Page's final ride. She and June, both milking it.

LUCY, I'M HOME! — SHE REACTS

Sigh. This one made me shmoopy. A lot shmoopy. Like . . . you better hope that vasectomy doctor didn't cut corners, shmoopy. OK, not THAT shmoopy. But I like having babies with you. A lot. And I hope that everyone reading this is feeling the same way. But about whoever THEY are having babies with. Which better not be with you.

LUCY, I'M HOME! — HE REACTS

Did we really both just end in all caps HOLY CRAPs? It was as if we planned this whole thing. Or that we're actually a somewhat decent couple.

Fortunately, I know that's indeed the case. We make a good pair, Page Fehling. And coincidentally, we also make good babies.

I'll never forget that Raleigh house. Less than 2,000 square feet. For a while, the changing table was in the . . . foyer. Our sunroom became the playroom. The living room became the dining room. And the dining room became the place where I remember first sitting down to write this book.

We've joked throughout about how long this book took to write, how much of a pain it was, how it hung over our heads. But I'd be lying if I said I wasn't a little nostalgic that we're hitting the finish line with this thing. "We've GOT to finish the book!" became our rallying cry, literally, for years, and while I'm proud of us, I'll miss the process.

So yeah, HOLY CRAP, parents and soon-to-be-parents. Here's a toast to you. *raises glass of Yellow Tail* Congratulations! If Page and I can make it, so can you. Good luck!

FIN

EPILOGUE & THANK YOUS

THAT WASN'T SO BAD AFTER ALL

He Said | *She Said*

Well, would you look at us, Page. Ten years after that first plus sign, and we finally finished this thing.

Who would have thought that with three kids and two jobs—one of which requires us to be vampires—this whole "writing a book" thing would be a little harder than we imagined.

Right. So . . .

Yes?

Remind me what goes in an epilogue?

OMG. This is where we tell people it's actually not that bad, that parenting is a true blessing, and to be on the lookout for our next book, coming NOT SOON.

Ah, that's right. And we thank people here, correct?

YES! Yes, we should probably definitely thank all of the people that helped us get excited about basically giving ourselves a fun version of grown-up homework . . . with a very lenient due date.

OK, I'll go first. I want to thank you, Page, for—

Stop.

No, seriously! While this book has been a source of contentment at times, and something we've considered shelving because it would only lead to frustration, the JOY of working on it with you far outweighs any negatives.

Awww, babe . . .

It's sort of like with our *Date Night with Jake and Page* podcast, where we get in arguments a lot over—

Quit while you're ahead. And that shameless podcast plug was NOT subtle.

Got it.

THEY SAID

No, but seriously, we have so many people to thank for helping make this book happen.

To Lisa Gallagher, our first and only agent. Thank you for believing in us and working hard trying to get someone to buy this. As with birth control . . . it can't work every time, but hey, it's worth a try!

To Jake's uncle, Sterling Watson. Thanks for taking the time to give us advice from an actual real-life author, and for introducing us to Lisa. Also for recommending we take out the line about Page's pee smelling like Honey Nut Cheerios. Thank you for sparing people from reading about that.

To our friends Lindsay, Ted, Beth, Brit, Penn, and Kim for reading early versions of the book and telling us when things weren't funny, or went too far. Just imagine what you'd have read about knowing none of them recommended nixing all the mucus plug references, the discharge lines, or the entire chapter on pregnant sex.

To our parents, who we literally wouldn't have been able to do this without. Because writing a book is hard to do when you don't even exist. Also really guys—THANK YOU for not reading Chapter 10. There were probably other snippets we should have warned you about. Too late now. And yes, again . . . that's what she (ahem . . . everyone reading this) said.

To Justin Batt for offering last minute publishing advice and for introducing us to Sara Stratton who helped bring this sucker across the goal line. She calls herself a book shepherd. We call her Marshawn Lynch. BEAST MODE.

And finally, to each other . . . for doing this pregnancy and parenting thing together and being willing to share all about it. Much like we felt every time we saw that line (or plus sign, or the words, "you're pregnant,". . . etc.), we still can't believe we did it.

THANK YOU!